Roll the Union On

A Pictorial History *of the* Southern Tenant Farmers' Union

As told by its co-founder, H. L. Mitchell

"To the disinherited belongs the future."

—Southern Tenant Farmers' Union
Ceremony of the Land

A Pictorial History
of the
Southern Tenant Farmers' Union

Roll the Union On

As told by its co-founder,
H. L. Mitchell

With an Introduction by
Orville Vernon Burton

Chicago
CHARLES H. KERR PUBLISHING COMPANY
Established 1886
1987

A full-length documentary film,
Our Land Too: The Legacy of the STFU,
based on this book, and issued concurrently with it,
has been produced by
KUDZU FILM PRODUCTIONS, INC.
of Huntsville, Alabama.

For information on the rental or purchase of this film,
contact any of the following:

STFU Association, Inc.
Box 2617, Montgomery AL 36105
(205)-265-4700

Kudzu Film Productions, Inc.
4415 Evangel Circle, Huntsville AL 35816
(205)-830-4332

National Sharecroppers Fund, Inc.
2124 Commonwealth Avenue, Charlotte NC 28205
(704)-334-3051

or the publisher of this book.

The Great Seal of the STFU,
reproduced on the title-page and elsewhere
throughout this book,
was designed by noted artist Janet Fraser
around 1937.

ISBN 0-88286-159-x paper
0-88286-160 cloth

CHARLES H. KERR PUBLISHING COMPANY
P.O. Box 914
Chicago IL 60690

ROLL THE UNION ON

Words by JOHN HANDCOX

With a steady beat

CHORUS

We're gon-na ' roll,——we're gon-na roll,——we're gon-na roll the u-nion on! We're gon-na roll,——we're gon-na roll,——we're gonna roll the u-nion on! If the boss is in the way we're gon-na roll it o - ver him, we're gon-na roll it o - ver him, we're gon-na roll it o - ver him. If the roll the u - nion on.

Blacks and Whites Unite: A Gathering of the STFU. (Photo by Louise Boyle)

Author's Foreword

This book is based on my earlier, full-length memoir, *Mean Things Happening in This Land*, published in 1979. The text has been substantially rewritten; much of it has been expanded and updated; and several entirely new sections have been added. *Roll the Union On* also includes far more photographs and other illustrations, and several additional songs and poems, as well as a list of books recommended for further reading.

Many people helped in the production of this book, above all my wife Dorothy Dowe Mitchell, the Treasurer of the STFU and its successors since 1943. I would especially like to thank Leona M. Torode for her generous assistance in putting together this succinct history. My friends at the Charles H. Kerr Publishing Company have also been helpful in many ways. Dave Roediger, Franklin Rosemont, Penelope Rosemont and the late Fred Thompson helped with the final editing, Lisa Oppenheim provided the design and layout, and Joel Williams contributed valuable technical assistance.

I've been ordering books from Charles H. Kerr for over fifty years now—since the very first days of the Southern Tenant Farmers' Union—and it is a pleasure to have this pictorial history issued under the imprint of this venerable cooperative, the oldest labor and socialist publishing house in the world.

H. L. Mitchell

Montgomery, Alabama
June 27, 1987

Introduction

I do not exaggerate when I say that H. L. Mitchell is a major leader of twentieth-century America, for he has championed the cause of farm laborers before every President from Franklin Roosevelt to Ronald Reagan. Mitchell's contributions to labor organization border on the legendary. H. L. Mitchell is a white southern radical who, in 1934, with black and white sharecroppers, organized a new movement—the Southern Tenant Farmers' Union (STFU) —to meet the needs of rural working people. Twenty years later the renowned labor leader, Walter Reuther of the United Auto Workers, proclaimed that Mitchell was "already a legend in the South when I was just a punk in an auto plant in Detroit."[1] A lifelong activist for black and white rural workers, this native-born southerner was honored by being named vice-president of the National Association for the Advancement of Colored People (NAACP) in 1948.

Surveying the transformation of agriculture in the southern United States, historian George Brown Tindall remarked that the delta town of Tyronza, Arkansas, was an improbable place for a Socialist Party local in 1932.[2] But the more one learns about nonconformist H. L. Mitchell, instigator of that local, the more one understands that improbable events occurred wherever he was involved.

Mitchell tried his hand at a variety of jobs, from bootlegging in prohibition days to sharecropping, before he found his avocation as farm labor organizer. Perhaps the story really began in 1917 when the eleven-year-old newspaper boy rode the train from Halls to Dyersburg, Tennessee and watched whites lynch a young black man. Searching for some way to understand the world around him, Mitch became what southerners called a "reading fool." A Norman Thomas socialist, Mitchell converted his pal Clay East to his way of thinking, and by the time of the 1932 presidential election, Tyronza residents had designated the area of town around Mitchell's dry-cleaning plant and East's filling station "Red Square." In 1934 the two spearheaded the interracial Southern Tenant Farmers' Union. To this organization Mitchell has devoted his life. Even today, when he talks about the union, there is a twinkle in his eye. With Mitchell's organizational skills and Clay East's packing a pistol as the duly elected township constable, the union thrived.

Louisiana sugarcane worker's house, 1960.

Through the STFU, Mitchell began a lifetime of lobbying the rich and powerful on behalf of America's have-nots. Thus, he tells moving stories of America's common folk as well as some of its most famous characters—Eleanor Roosevelt, A. Philip Randolph, Helen Gahagan Douglas, to mention only a few. In 1984 National Public Radio carried a report on the STFU's golden anniversary reunion at Little Rock. The commentator noted that ''Historians say that the Southern Tenant Farmers' Union helped poor southern farm families more than anything since the Homestead Act (1862).'' By protesting sharecropper evictions, organizing strikes and lobbying for federal legislation to improve agricultural conditions in the South, and by doing this with the support and cooperation of both black and white farm families, southern radicals fought the system. Infused with the ''Social Gospel'' and at times with the teachings of Marx, they sought to break the power of the plantation barons. Along with strikes to raise wages, their most successful effort culminated in the formation of the Delta Co-operative Farm at Rochdale, Mississippi, formed by tenants evicted from Arkansas plantations for joining the STFU. This project became the model for the Farm Security Adminstration, created as a result of the growing concern for the plight of the southern tenant farmer.

This book's concentration on rural America fills a gap; by and large, scholars interested in labor history have directed their attention to industrialization, immigrant communities, and urban areas, generally ignoring the problems of twentieth century American workers toiling on the land.[3] *Roll the Union On* portrays, with words and pictures, the conditions and hardships that rural farm families faced, and the STFU's activities on their behalf. It vividly chronicles the problems encountered by an integrated southern union in the 1930s when segregation was a way of life in the South.

What made H. L. Mitchell tick? Somewhat contrary, Mitchell does not quite fit the the profile of the ''average'' southern reformer described in the history books. Most were steeped in the Social Gospel movement, but Mitchell,

the agnostic son and grandson of preachers, came at the problems of rural America from an economic perspective. Evelyn Smith Munro, an STFU office secretary, described the young organizer:

Harry Leland Mitchell, always thereafter to be known as Mitch. . .was young, with a charming, unselfconscious boyishness. . . . He was also the Man with the Hoe, Billy the Kid, and Abraham Lincoln, with a little of Jesse James thrown in. His drawl was authentic if his simplicity was not. . . . Mitchell's imagination. . .always kept him one idea ahead of the rest of the union leadership. He had a natural-born knack for publicity. . . . Mitch couldn't spell and his grammar wasn't anything to write home about, but he knew what would make people respond—whether to a union handbill, an appeal for funds, or an expose of government ineptitude. . . . His work, his recreation and his consuming interest was the Union and the Socialist Party.[4]

Mitchell was a mover; he made things happen. Frequently he was embroiled in turmoil. Whether AFL-CIO president George Meany approved or not (and most frequently he did not), Mitchell did what he thought was right for his agricultural union. His vision of cooperative farming for black and white tenants, sharecroppers and wage-laborers stirred his Christian mentor and friend, ''Buck'' Kester, to explain that ''Mitchell *had a dream.*'' The STFU lived by the creed that Mitchell made his own: ''Nothing will win the battle quicker than by having members of all races, creeds and colors united in one strong union.''

To his story, and that of seven blacks and eleven whites in Tyronza, contemporary historians are now turning to understand the beginnings of the organized farm-labor movement and the origins of the modern-day civil rights movement. Somewhere between the economically inspired Populist revolt of the 1890s and Martin Luther King, Jr's religiously inspired dream, came Mitchell and the STFU, with the dream of black and white poor people uniting against the rich and powerful. Beyond the anecdotal, the history of ordinary southern sharecroppers, black and white, is like the history of all inarticulate people—slaves, peasants, sharecroppers alike: shadowy but important groups who leave few or no written records. They surge unexpectedly onto the historical stage during an agrarian protest to provide a colorful melee, wreck the scenery, and then retire to the wings, leaving few tracks for the historian to follow. But thanks to Mitchell's careful record-keeping, historians have been left with fertile fields for research.

While Mitch likes to "tell it like it is," this is by no means an objective history. But his bias is a welcome correction to much of American history which has been interpreted through the experiences of its elite. As the twentieth century nears an end, more historians are looking to the 1930s and '40s as an era to research, and the story of the STFU is a particularly important chapter. Already, a superb monograph has been written by Donald H. Grubbs, *Cry from the Cotton: The Southern Tenant Farmers' Union and the New Deal.*[5] Moreover, as historians search for the wellsprings of the modern civil rights movement, many stress the historical significance of this first fully-integrated interracial movement in the cottonfields of the South. Economist John Kenneth Galbraith believes that the civil rights movement started with the interracial STFU. Mitchell's autobiography, Galbraith has written, "in a very real sense tells where civil and political rights in the South began."[6]

Indeed, H. L. Mitchell was one of several idealistic reformers working in the South for economic and racial justice in the 1930s and '40s, a group that Anthony Dunbar appropriately labeled "Southern Radicals and Prophets" going *Against the Grain.*[7] In an eloquent testimonial to these noble warriors, Thomas A. Krueger, another historian of the modern South, recently concluded:

They did not fail for want of trying. This may be the only group of radicals in modern American history who stayed active until death parted them from the struggle. Nobody quit. Nobody sold out. Perhaps there is something good to be said for a fighting Christian faith after all.[8]

To paraphrase Mark Twain, reports of the death of the STFU are exaggerated. As it is too early for H. L. Mitchell's obituary, it is also too soon for an epitaph for the STFU. As long as Mitchell lives, so does the STFU. Just as historians are mistaken to view the conflicts of the 1930s as an aberration in the smooth flow of the consensus in American history,[9] so too this memoir suggests that there may be more continuity to the Left and to American reform movements than historians have acknowledged. Mitch, the ironic raconteur, is still going strong. He still exudes charm and enthusiasm. This seemingly tireless reformer is a spellbinding and energetic speaker and writer who brings history alive through observation and anecdote. It is an eyeopener to stroll the decades where he is both actor and historian.

In this era in which America has been reluctant to believe in real heroes, it is important that people know about the life of this extraordinary man. I once asked Mitch why he did it—what motivated him and kept him going. In good southern storytelling manner he told me what his friend, Clay East, suggested: that Mitch probably did not have any better sense than to keep on fighting. Yet it was a different kind of fighting than East himself would do. Rather than fighting a mob with gun, knife or fist, Mitchell would run—not because he was afraid, but so that he could come back to fight another day. Mitchell himself would not analyze his motivation, but he did say that he had never been bored. And his story, told here, will never bore, either.

Orville Vernon Burton

University of Illinois,
Urbana-Champaign

NOTES

I have benefitted from the suggestions of James Barrett, Georganne Burton, Thomas A. Krueger, and Stanley Nadel.

1. H. L. Mitchell, *Mean Things Happening in This Land: The Life and Times of H. L. Mitchell, Co-founder of the Southern Tenant Farmers' Union* (Montclair, NJ: Allanheld, Osmun & Co., 1979), 240.

2. George Brown Tindall, *The Emergence of the New South, 1913-1945*, vol. 10 in *A History of the South*, edited by Wendell Holmes Stephenson and E. Merton Coulter (Baton Rouge: Louisiana State University Press, 1967), 417.

3. See Robert P. Swierenga's call for the study of rural history, "Agriculture and Rural Life: The New Rural History," in *Ordinary People and Everyday Life: Perspectives on the New Social History*, edited by James B. Gardner and George Rollie Adams (Nashville: Association for State and Local History, 1983), 91-113.

4. Evelyn Smith Munro, *Memoirs*, unpublished manuscript in the Papers of the Southern Tenant Farmers' Union, Southern Historical Collection, University of North Carolina, Chapel Hill.

5. Donald H. Grubb, *Cry from the Cotton: The Southern Tenant Farmers' Union and the New Deal* (Chapel Hill: University of North Carolina Press, 1971).

6. Quotation from letter to H. L. Mitchell from John Kenneth Galbraith, cited on the brochure, "What They Say About H. L. Mitchell and his Book, *Mean Things Happening in This Land.*"

7. Anthony P. Dunbar, *Against the Grain: Southern Radicals and Prophets, 1929-1959* (Charlottesville: University Press of Virginia, 1981).

8. Review of Dunbar's *Against the Grain* by Thomas A. Krueger in *The Journal of American History*, vol. 69, 1 (June 1982), 199-200.

9. Eugene Lyons, *The Red Decade* (Indianapolis: Bobbs-Merrill, 1941).

Growing Up in the Rural South

The Lynching

It was a cold, dark and damp day in December of 1917 when I, Harry Leland Mitchell, a white boy of eleven years, stood on a railway platform in my home town, Halls, Tennessee, awaiting the arrival of a special excursion train to a lynching to be held twelve miles away. In less than an hour the train, carrying upwards of 200 men, women and children, arrived in Dyersburg. The cars were fast emptied as the excited passengers rushed to the county courthouse a few blocks away. Chained to an iron post on the courthouse lawn was Scott Lignon, accused of attempted rape of a middle-aged white woman, at whose home he had delivered groceries the day before. Arrested and jailed, Lignon had been turned over to the mob estimated at more than 500 people there to see the lynching.

Scott Lignon was crying, "Oh God, is there no help for the widow's son?" I pushed through the waiting crowd to the front row. Two pot-bellied white men in charge of the proceedings were waiting for the crowd to assemble. One said to the other, "We can't do this, that boy is a Mason." (The Masonic fraternal order was very strong in those days.) The other replied, "He's just a nigger Mason, let's burn him." With that, a match was put to the wooden shavings and goods boxes saturated with gasoline that were piled high around the young black man. The flames rose high, and the odor of burning flesh permeated the air. Scott Lignon's body slumped, held up by the chains, as his life expired. Nauseated, I pushed back through the crowd and ran to the railway station, where I lay down on the cold wooden platform, sick at the sight I had seen.

It was the only lynching I was ever to witness, but family and friends had previously told me of other such episodes in their gory details. This experience undoubtedly helped shape the life I was to follow in the future.

Little Cotton Picker (photo by Louise Boyle)

Becoming a Socialist in Moscow
(Moscow, Tennessee, that is)

I attended school three to four months twice a year, the sessions being widely separated. Between sessions, from the time I was eight, I worked in the fields, earning as little as fifty cents for a workday of from twelve to fourteen hours (from *can see* to *can't see*). I weeded cotton with a long-handled hoe in the spring, then picked cotton in the fall. I did not get much learning.

One day I read an advertisement in the daily newspaper which said, "If you oppose Evolution, you should know what it is. Send us $1.00 and we will send you twenty of the Little Blue Books listed below." The Little Blue Books were condensations of the classics and books on topical subjects like *Evolution Made Plain* and *What Is Socialism?* Over the next few years, I acquired nearly 500 titles.

The publisher was E. Haldeman-Julius of Girard, Kansas. The books were a part of the education process started by the Socialist movement. They were first printed on the presses of the *Appeal to Reason*, a Socialist Party newspaper. The circulation of the *Appeal* was greater than that of the *Saturday Evening Post,* prior to World War I. Will Durant's *Story of Philosophy* was first published in a Little Blue Book edition, and I read it.

Three years after the lynching, I heard my first socialist speech, delivered by Dr. John Morris, an itinerant veterinarian who followed the race tracks. Morris spoke on a streetcorner in Moscow, a rural town in Tennessee, and I heard him say, "I would rather be Eugene V. Debs in the Federal Penitentiary in Atlanta, than Woodrow Wilson in the White House in Washington, D.C." Not understanding, I followed the horse doctor around the town asking him ques-

tions. I became a socialist. I urged every man I met to vote for Gene Debs who stood for a new day and a better life for all such as we were.

Four years later, still too young to vote, I campaigned for Robert M. LaFollette, the Progressive Party candidate. I cast my first ballot in Arkansas in 1928 for Norman Thomas, the Socialist candidate for president, who was to run six times for the office.

Bootlegger, Student and Married Man

In Colliersville, another rural town also east of Memphis, I became the town bootlegger while working as the delivery boy for a grocery store and meat market. I had a readymade market. There was a band of Irish horse traders who wintered each year in Colliersville. They would drink anything, including lemon extract used in baking cakes. Jamaica Ginger, which had a high alcoholic content, was also a favorite drink. One day a moonshiner delivered a keg of whiskey to me, hiding it in a barn. There were no bottles. I was out searching the bushes along the street from home to downtown for empties. The city policeman, who knew what was going on, followed me on my rounds, seeking the liquid evidence. Although he had no evidence, he threatened to arrest me.

The Irish horse traders declared they had never in their lives bought whiskey from me. The storekeeper and the butcher also lied to save their delivery boy, but ordered me, the enterprising entrepreneur, to end my profitable and illegal undertaking of selling bootleg whiskey.

On moving back to Halls, Tennessee, my birthplace, I re-entered school, and was allowed to rejoin my former classmates now in high school, without the required credit. My favorite teacher, Elizabeth Batey, in her early twenties, became interested in the

Home of H. L. Mitchell, near Halls, Tennessee, circa 1917.

young rebel and his wild ideas about atheism, evolution and socialism. Controversies daily disrupted her English and History classes, until the principal ordered the cessation of such unseemly carryings-on in the classroom. Thereafter Miss Batey and I engaged in our earnest discussions while walking home from school together, and sometimes far into the evening at the teachers' residence, where all the unmarried teachers lived. This was very stimulating to me.

Soon after finishing high school, I got a job with an engineering survey party working on the U.S. highways being built in Tennessee. After about a year the survey party transferred to East Tennessee, 400 miles away. By that time there were two girl-friends, and I didn't want to leave them.

Lois had a talent for singing and playing the piano. The other girl was Lyndell, whom I had met on a double date. About a year older than I was, and much more mature, Dell was the eldest of a family of thirteen children. Her father, Sam Carmack, was a rural mail carrier and farm owner at Curve, a community a few miles away. On the day after Christmas in 1926, Dell and I were married by a minister of the Church of Christ. Dell was teaching school, seventy-five pupils of all ages and grades, for the sum of $60 a month. I couldn't find a job, so during our first year we newlyweds made a sharecrop on the Carmack farm. Our income from the sharecrop was $185 for the year 1927.

Sharecropping in Arkansas

Jim Mitchell, my father, then a barber in Arkansas, urged the would-be farmer to come to Tyronza and farm where he could make two bales of cotton

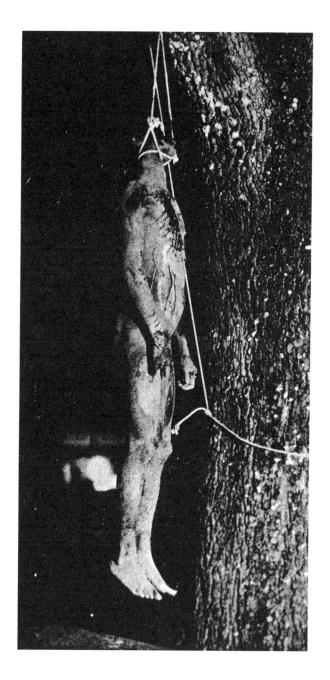

The Lynching of Claude Neal, October 1934. Howard Kester, investigator for the NAACP, bought this picture from a local entrepreneur.

Left: *Cottonfield in Arkansas.* (Photo by Dorothea Lange)
Above: *Cotton pickers weigh in.* (Photo by Louise Boyle)

to the acre. What Jim didn't say, or perhaps didn't know, was that "The landlord got one bale, and the boll weevil the other."

Late in the year 1927, I went to Tyronza by train. I borrowed my father's Model T Ford and found someone to drive me out to the plantation where I had been offered a house and land on which to make a crop in 1928.

The gravel road to the plantation ended at the company store. Black families lived on one side, and white families on the other, of the impassable road. At the far end of the road there were some unoccupied houses, of which I had been told to take my pick. At the first house I pushed open the front door, which almost fell off its insecure hinges. There was a room for sleeping and a room for cooking and eating. The house was made of green lumber that had warped in the hot delta sun, and daylight could be seen through all of the walls from the inside. It had a tin roof as protection from rain, and I could imagine the rain drumming above the heads of people trying to sleep under it.

Outside was the water supply—a pipe driven into the ground to bring up the shallow surface water, with a suction pump that no longer worked. A few feet distant was the outdoor two-holer johnny, filled with human excrement. The other empty houses were no better. From occupied houses, smoke arose from tin pipes above the front room, and little children, black and white alike, watched the newcomers from behind dirty windowpanes.

Returning to Tyronza, I told my father that I was going back to Tennessee where things were more civilized.

Cotton picking in Arkansas. (Photo by Louise Boyle)

Storefront of business operated by H. L. Mitchell (wearing tie) in 1934.

Big Businessman in a Small Town

Jim the barber then challenged his son to take over the pressing machine in the back of the barber shop and make a living pressing clothes. Soon my family and I joined the elders in Tyronza, Arkansas. "Tyronza Cleaners, H. L. Mitchell, Prop." was painted on the door of the shop and on the side of a panel-type truck. With a helper who could drive the truck, I was scouring the countryside, seeking clothing to be dry-cleaned.

Never discriminating where a dollar was to be made, we called at the homes of planters, riding bosses or sharecroppers. If there was work to be had, I was after business. Prospering, the Tyronza Cleaners expanded. New-fangled dry-cleaning machines were acquired.

Some of the "upper class" women of the town called upon me threatening to withhold their patronage if I didn't stop cleaning clothing that belonged to those plantation "Nigrahs." I advised them that I had two cleaning machines—one for white folks' clothes, the other for the colored folks' clothes—and that Johnny, my black helper, pressed the black folks' clothing. I assured the "ladies" that everything in my shop was kept segregated. There was not a word of truth in any of it, but the townspeople were satisfied that the southern way of life was fully preserved by the Tyronza Cleaners.

The Man from Island 37

Another lucrative business was soon added—that of taking orders for made-to-measure suits for men's tailoring plants in Chicago, Cincinnati and Baltimore. I got 33⅓% on every order I sent in. A small deposit was required.

One day a man stopped at the barber shop to get his long hair trimmed, and came on to the cleaning plant next door. Mr Guy Thomas ordered a suit and an overcoat and insisted on paying cash in advance for the full amount of over $100. While taking Thomas' measurements, I asked him if he was a cotton planter. "Hell no!" said the customer. "Over on Island No. 37 we just grow some corn and make it into whiskey." Those were Prohibition days. The Constitution of the United States had been amended to outlaw the making, selling or drinking of any kind of hard liquor, beer or wine.

Thomas invited me to come for a visit the following Sunday, as he was sure some of the other boys on the little island in the big Mississippi would want to order suits and overcoats, and their wives might have some dry-cleaning business for me.

With my new helper, Clifford, I drove over to the river levee some thirty miles away and forded the old river cut-off that formed Island No. 37. As we started up a narrow winding road, a big black fellow stepped out of the bushes with a rifle cradled in his arms, and said, "Whar you goin,' white folks? If I wus you, I'd just turn right round and go back the way you come." I pointed to the sign on my truck, but the big fellow was not impressed, as he could not read. But when I insisted I had been invited to visit Mr Thomas, the black man led the way up to Guy Thomas' house, and when Guy came out to welcome his guests, disappeared back into the canebrake.

I learned that nearly every man on Island No. 37 had served a prison term, and some were escaped convicts. A keg of the island's best whiskey was brought out, and the men started to tell stories, sipping whiskey while sitting on the porch, or hunkered down on the ground. Several orders were taken for made-to-measure suits and overcoats. The women and children arrived. A picnic was spread on the ground, and all gathered round to eat fried chicken, ham and catfish. Clothing in need of cleaning was brought out, and the two cleaners made a cleaning.

We left at sundown. Guy Thomas brought out two bottles of Island No. 37's best whiskey, one for the cleaners and the other for Jim the barber back in Tyronza. I offered to pay for the liquor but was told that my money was counterfeit on Island No. 37. Thomas suggested that we just do a bit of advertising for him. "Tell folks you know that whiskey from Island No. 37 is every bit as good as that made by Ike Williams on the St. Francis River" (bottled under Ike's label, in spite of the U.S. Constitution's prohibiting the sale of it).

As long as I remained in business I would make a trip at least once a month to see my friends on No. 37. I nearly always found some work to do. The ex-cons weren't bothered with preachers out to save their souls. The womenfolk worried about the children not getting much learning, but they were free of most of the evils of plantation life.

Some time after the union got started, a flood came and Guy Thomas and his pals had to leave old No. 37. Thomas and a few of the No. 37ers went to Oklahoma. Thomas became an STFU organizer. He could tell many tales of his exploits, and those of his friends. One of the best was about a dog named "old Fuzzy." It seems that Guy and a couple of other fellows were down on the Red River, where they had

*Sharecropper Housing. (*Photo by Howard Kester)

regularly been dynamiting fish. This particular time, Old Fuzzy had followed him, and when Guy threw a stick of dynamite into the stream, Old Fuzzy—who had been trained to retrieve things—jumped in after the dynamite. Here came Old Fuzzy, returning the explosive. Guy took off through the woods, yelling loudly, "Call Old Fuzzy, call Old Fuzzy!" Poor Old Fuzzy never delivered the dynamite. Its explosion the woodland attracted the attention of a Game Warden on the prowl, searching for the men who were illegally stunning the fish with explosives and sel-

ling them in Muskogee and other towns. Guy and his pals claimed that Old Fuzzy had just picked up the dynamite, and Fuzzy wasn't there to dispute the claim, so the Game Warden had no evidence.

Several years later a man came out of the crowd of migrant workers at a union meeting in California, and said, "Hello there, Mitch. Don't you remember me? I am Guy Thomas from Island No. 37." Guy was not much older than I was, and may still be out there somewhere, peddling whiskey, dynamiting fish, or just talking union talk.

Revolt of the Sharecroppers

The Southern Tenant Farmers' Union:
Rural America's First Fully-Integrated Union

The New Deal in Agriculture got under way in the summer of 1933. Sharecroppers and planters plowed under every third row of cotton, because the government said this would raise prices. Each producer was to be paid a subsidy for plowing under a third of his crop the first year, and for reducing his acreage by forty per cent the second year. The government sent each plantation owner or operator a check, and he was supposed to share it with the sharecroppers. In over half the cases, the sharecroppers did not get a dime of the government money. If they protested, they were evicted from the land. (See the transcript of the *March of Time* newsreel, "The Land of Cotton," August 1936.)

In July of 1934, eleven white men and seven black men met at the Fairview schoolhouse south of Tyronza. My fellow businessman, Henry Clay East, and I were at the meeting. As we came in, Alvin Nunnally, who was acting as chairman, said, "If we do like some of you men say, form a necktie party and go out and get some planters like Hiram Norcross, we will all swing for it." He continued by saying they needed a legal organization for all sharecroppers, something like the Farmers' Educational and Cooperative Union of America (FECUA).

A decision was then taken to form such an organization, and the question next arose whether there should be one union for white folks and another for the black folks. A grizzly old sharecropper, Burt Williams, said that he and his pappy rode with the Ku Klux Klan and they drove the last Republican officeholders out of adjoining Crittenden County. *But*, he added, the time had come to forget those things and have one union for sharecroppers, both black and white. Pointing to Rev. C. H. Smith, sitting over to one side with the group of black sharecroppers, he said, "This man is my nearest neighbor. We live in the same kind of

Refused permission to meet in town, the STFU holds a meeting on the railroad tracks in February 1935. (Photo by Howard Kester)

23

house, we work for the same plantation owner. Our wives sit on the back porches and talk, drink coffee together, and when we run out of something, we borrow from each other. No man ever had a better neighbor than we do in C. H. Smith and family.''

Burt Williams asked the black folks to say how they felt, but none of them would say a word; not even Preacher Smith would respond. Finally, a tall, big black man arose. He was Isaac Shaw. In a booming voice Ike said, ''I think we are doing the right thing. We have decided to have a legal organization, and that all sharecroppers, black and white alike, are to be members. I think this organization will stand for all time to come if we accept these principles.''

Ike Shaw said he had been a member of the Farmers and Farm Laborers Association in nearby Philips County nearly fifteen years before. The Association had been wiped out in the Elaine Massacre. Isaac Shaw was an imposing personality. He had lived for some years on a plantation in Mississippi, as a kind of companion to a well-educated white owner (thought to be Will Percy, a liberal for those days, who wrote *Lanterns on the Levee*). Shaw had learned to speak clearly and to use good English, but he never learned to read or write. That night someone had to witness his mark on the application card.

I spoke up for the first time that night, and said, ''This time it is going to be different. We white men are going to be in the front, and when shooting starts, we will be the first to go down. But you know, we have Clay East here with us. He is the law in Tyronza township, and he can protect us all.''

Another man said if we have two unions, then the boss will get rid of us white folks and take the colored in our places, or do the same with them. This decided the issue. Clay East said, ''Well, if you folks mean business, let's get going. Mitch has some cards

here. Put your name on one. If you can't write, make your mark, and I will fill out the rest for you.'' Every man there signed, and each man promised to help.

I sent out word to all the socialists in the South about the founding of the Tenant Farmers' Union, and invited young and old to come help organize.

First to respond was Rev. Ward H. Rodgers, a young Methodist minister from Pumpkin Center, Arkansas. Ward abandoned his church, and did not bring any of his parishoners' money with him. (They had none.) Rodgers afterward said he was a ''Circuit Walking Preacher,'' as he had no means of transportation to get from one of his churches to another. Soon after Rodgers' arrival, C. H. Smith had a meeting at a church-house near Gilmore, in nearby Crittenden County, and he asked Ward Rodgers to go with him to the meeting. The plantation riding bosses had been alerted, and Rodgers and Smith were caught before they could get to the meeting place. Riders and deputy sheriffs let Rodgers the white preacher go, but they put the black preacher, Smith, in jail, and beat him with rubber hoses, trying to make him tell the names of the union members in Crittenden County. Smith refused to talk.

I sent a telegram to the American Civil Liberties Union in New York, asking for the names of lawyers who could get the union man out of jail. The ACLU sent names of three lawyers in Memphis. East and I went over to see them. One, a judge, was ill, and another had just left for a job with the New Deal in Washington. The remaining one, Abe Waldauer, agreed to meet with us, but said, ''I lost all my bravery in the Argonne Forest with that Lost Battallion in World War I, and here is one Jewish lawyer who is not about to go to Arkansas to get a Nigra preacher out of jail.''

Clay East

Far left: *STFU co-founder Isaac Shaw, spokesman for black people at the Union's first meeting on July 13, 1934.* Above: *Fairview School (near Tyronza, Arkansas) where the STFU's first meeting was held. Eleven white and seven black sharecroppers met to found this historic movement.* Left: *Zita Baker and Naomi Mitchison, women from across the sea, led protest march in Marked Tree, Arkansas, in 1935.*

Sharecroppers assemble in Marked Tree, Arkansas, to hear report of the STFU delegation to Washington. (Photo by Howard Kester)

The STFU Hires Its First Lawyer

We went to see C. T. Carpenter in Marked Tree, Arkansas, and asked him if he would get Smith out of jail. The lawyer replied, "Yes, but I must be retained by your union, and my fee is $100." Though the union treasury was empty, I hired him on the spot. I didn't have $5 of my own, but I understood what the distinguished Virginian was saying—that he must be able to say in court that he had been retained by the union to represent C. H. Smith.

Carpenter had a date set for the hearing, and told us to get a few of the white union members to come to the courthouse. They were not to do or to say anything, just be there in silent support of Preacher Smith. On the appointed day, two cars and a truck were loaded with white union members who proceeded to the trial in Marion. Many of them carried walking-sticks, for self-defense—just in case—but leaned on them as if crippled.

Lawyer Carpenter made his plea, and C. H. Smith was paroled without bond in Mr Carpenter's care. The union men accompanied Smith back to the Fairview School, where a great crowd of sharecroppers, their wives and children were waiting. Smith was the guest of honor that day, and he described how the white union men and the union lawyer had come to his rescue.

Soon after the first meeting, the union was incorporated under Arkansas law in the name of the Southern Tenant Farmers' Union. When Dr William R. Amberson read the first draft of Union By-Laws, he remarked to East and me, "Boys, you are trying to have the Revolution incorporated." The attorney for the union, C. T. Carpenter, soon filed a lawsuit to enforce the rights of sharecroppers under the Agricultural Adjustment Act.

Cotton Pickers!
S T R I K E !
For $1 per 100 lbs
Refuse to pick a boll for less!

Strike on every farm or plantation where cotton is being picked for wages!

Accept No Less Than The Union Prices—— $1 per 100 lbs

Strike Call Effective TODAY

Special Committee
SOUTHERN TENANT FARMERS UNION

See Instructions for local strikes Committees

Please Pass This On

The STFU's first strike handbill.

Ward H. Rodgers presiding at an STFU open-air meeting. Threatened with lynching, he responded: "I can lead a lynch mob to lynch any cotton plantation owner in Poinsett County, Arkansas." Over a thousand hats were thrown into the air. Rodgers was thereupon jailed and charged with criminal anarchy, blasphemy and calling a black man "Mister."

"The Land of Cotton"

Partial transcript of *March of Time* newsreel
(August 1936)

In all the United States, there is no parallel to the economic bondage in which cotton holds the South. Victims of this one-crop system are the five and one-half million white folk, three million Negroes, tenant farmers, sharecroppers, laborers who own no land themselves, but farm sixty percent of the South's twenty-seven million acres of cotton. Victims, too, and completely dependent on the cotton-belt's one source of income, are the planter-landlords.

Landlord to sharecropper: I know times are hard, and I know the pickin's are far from plenty, but it's the system that is all wrong. It has been handed down to us through generations. It can't be corrected overnight. You don't think I'm getting rich, do you?

Sharecropper: No, sir.

Commentator: A surplus of thirteen million bales, a whole year's production, piled up in southern warehouses. Then the New Deal stepped in, ordered every third row of the new crop plowed under. The next year increasing the program to cut forty percent of all cotton acreage. Nine-hundred thousand men and women were let off the land. Vast sums were paid out in benefits, but some of the sharecroppers failed to receive their part of the government's benefit checks, and their protest reverberated in Washington's Department of Agriculture, where three officials were fired, among them Gardner Jackson of the AAA [Agricultural Adjustment Administration].

Jackson to newspapermen: Well, one of the reasons we were fired is because Jerome Frank, Lee Pressman, and some of the rest of us tried to see to it that these sharecroppers got something approaching a square deal.

Newspaperman: What percentage of the sharecroppers do you figure got gypped?

Jackson: In darn near half the cases, the sharecroppers didn't get a nickel of the benefit payments. The landlords pocketed it all, but actually politics is in back of it. It would be political suicide to go against the planters. They are the Democrats who have the real power in the South.

Commentator: Echoing across Arkansas are the first rumblings of revolt in the Southland.

Young sharecropper: You have been sharecropping all your life and you haven't got a thing to show for it.

Speaker: We can't live on seventy-five cents a day, and I defy any planter to show me how a man can live on that wage. *[Applause]*

Blackstone (singing): Let's build the Southern Tenant Farmers Union and make our country worthwhile to live in.

Commentator: The headquarters of the Southern Tenant Farmers Union is set up in Memphis, just across the Mississippi River from the troubled region. As membership swelled to ten thousand, to twenty-five thousand, the cotton-farmers demanded that the planters sign written contracts to pay wages of $1.50 for a ten-hour day, and recognize their right to organize. Soon many a country road was peopled with families wandering aimlessly, some homeless because of curtailed production, others evicted by planters for joining Union activities. Then the Union called its members to unite for the cottonfields' first strike.

Sharecropper organizer: Let them jail us if they want to. We'll fill every jail in Arkansas, but get out of the fields, and stay out until the bosses give in.

(Singing of "We Shall Not Be Moved.")

Commentator: Faced with the prospect of ruined profits, the Arkansas planters closed ranks.

Planter: If they haven't got enough sense to know that this Union business is going to make things worse, we've got to teach them.

(Cars of men driving down the road.)

(Claude Williams and Willie Sue Blagden are stopped on road.)

Commentator: News of the investigating expedition from Tennessee had already reached planters in the little Arkansas town of Earle.

Williams: What do you men want?

Planters: All right, now get going down that highway.

Williams led by men; one remarks: We have had enough of you Yankee agitators coming down here stirring up trouble.

(Then, having beaten Williams, the men come for Willie Sue.)

Planters: All right, come on out. You're next, sister.

Commentator: The next day the violence in the Blagden-Williams investigation came into sharp focus for the entire nation.

(Newspaper headlines—'Eastern Arkansas Planters Flog Woman and Man.")

Commentator: From Arkansas' capital at Little Rock, Governor J. Marion Futrell speaks out in defense of the planters.

Governor: I deny that there is any peonage in Arkansas, and I defy any one of these outside agitators to prove that there is.

Commmentator: According to the Arkansas Governor, it is not the planter who is at fault in the Southland, but the one-crop system which has both planter and sharecropper in peonage. Gone are the days when U.S. cotton dominated the world's supply. Foreign countries stepped up production and took U.S. markets while U.S. planters were being forced to curtail their production. Gone too are King Cotton's traditional boundaries where southern wealth was born. Today one-third of all U.S. cotton grows in the new fertile stretches of Texas and Oklahoma, where large-scale industrialized farming can produce cotton forty percent cheaper than in the Old South.

(Church scene—singing of "Holy, holy, holy.")

Commentator: It is plain today that planter and sharecropper alike are the economic slaves of the South's one-crop system that only basic change can restore the one-time peace and prosperity of the Kingdom of Cotton. Time marches on.

Sharecroppers Go to Washington

A delegation of five was sent to Washington to enlist the aid of Secretary of Agriculture Henry Wallace, considered a great liberal. Two white and two black sharecroppers and I made a non-stop automobile trip 955 miles to Washington. During the second night on the road we lost our way and sought information at a building with lights on near the highway. An elderly man was sitting next to a wood-burning heater. Young men were sleeping in bunks, but we soon learned that we were not in one of the New Deal's C.C.C. (Civilian Conservation Corps) camps, but a prison camp. My companion, Walter Moskop, and I did not bother to find the gate by which we had entered, but rushed out, climbed a fence, and landed in a briarpatch on the other side. We ran to the car, and told the others, "Let's get the hell out of here—that's a convict camp, and they may think we are escaping prisoners."

The delegation arrived in Washington at an early hour the next morning. Just as the sun was coming up, we knocked on the huge doors at the U.S. Department of Agriculture. An unarmed night watchman told us that the workers would arrive around eight o'clock, and officials, like the Secretary, around nine. Seeing the Washington Monument in the distance, we went over to see that, but found it closed, with a sign on the door saying, "Open at 10:00."

Giving the USDA people time to settle down to work, the delegation returned to find a guard now sitting at a desk near the open doorway, who told us that we would find the Secretary's office in Room 204 up the stairs. I told the receptionist that we had come from Arkansas to see Mr Wallace. She asked if the group had an appointment. Unprepared for this, I hesitated, and black sharecropper "Brit" McKin-

ney, the STFU Vice-President, came to my rescue, saying "Miss, if Mr Wallace is busy right now, we will all just sit down here and wait for him. We have come a thousand miles, and have just got to see the Secretary of Agriculture." This was likely the first sit-down ever to occur in the Department of Agriculture.

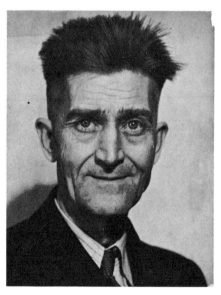

Left: *Sharecroppers storm the courthouse in Harrisburg, Arkansas, early 1935, demanding relief.* (Photo by Howard Kester)   Above: *J. R. Butler, President of the STFU, 1935-1942.* (Photo by Dorothea Lange)

The Rev. A. B. Brookins, STFU Chaplain and Song Leader. His favorite song was "Norman Thomas is our leader, we shall not be moved." Brookins' home was machinegunned, and his daughter, who was hiding under the bed, was hit by a ricocheting bullet.

Soon Mr Wallace came out to speak to the group and promised to send a special investigator to Arkansas. The person later sent was a woman lawyer who had just come to work in the USDA legal section. Mary Connor Myers had previously been on the Al Capone case. The Chicago gangster was convicted of violating the income tax law, just as was Ted Agnew, Vice-President of the United States, forty years later.

Elated that the Secretary of Agriculture was going to investigate the plight of the sharecroppers under the New Deal, the delegation left Washington. I sent a telegram to Ward Rodgers, telling him to call a meeting of union members. Some days later, over 500 sharecroppers turned out to hear the report of their first delegation to Washington.

The little lodge-hall would seat no more than 200, so the meeting was held on the town square in Marked Tree, Arkansas. Rodgers, who was acting as chairman of the meeting, made some opening remarks, and said he could lead a lynch mob and lynch any planter in the county. Hats went up, as men called out with a roar, "Come on, boys, let's go get them!" Realizing that a mistake was being made, I spoke up, and told the crowd in detail about the success of the delegation's meeting with Wallace. I closed with this: " Ward Rodgers is staying at my house, and if those sons of bitches get their heads in pillowcases and come around looking for him, they will get the hell shot out of them." Rodgers was arrested and charged with anarchy, blasphemy, and calling a Negro "Mister," then hurried away for safe-keeping in jail in Jonesboro, thirty miles away. The Establishment was fearful that the sharecroppers would rise in revolt if they arrested and jailed both of us. Instead, they planned my assassination, as we shall see.

"The Gene Debs of Dixie"

Howard Kester, Socialist and Social Gospel Minister, arrived in Arkansas in early 1935. One of the founders of the Committee of Southern Churchmen, who believed in the rights of all men, Kester became the friend, advisor, outside contact-man and spokesman for the STFU. His first job was to help free union men jailed on trumped-up charges.

Kester had run for Congress as a Socialist in his home town of Nashville. He had taken part in a coal-miners' strike. There he had seen his friend, the leader of the miners, shot down in the streets of Wilder, Tennessee. He had investigated lynchings for the NAACP, risking his life many times. He was making a speech at a little church in Arkansas when it was raided by plantation thugs. People were beaten with axe-handles and pistol-whipped. Quick thinking saved Howard Kester and the union lawyer from lynching that day. Kester was at Birdsong, Arkansas with Norman Thomas when a band of plantation riders and deputy sheriffs broke up a meeting at a local church. Kester became the amanuensis of the sharecroppers, writing the first book about the members of the STFU. Published in 1936, *Revolt Among the Sharecroppers* is still a standard work that depicts the early struggles of the workers to organize.

In later life, Kester became a professor and retired as the Dean of Students at the Montreat Anderson College, near Black Mountain, North Carolina, where he died in 1977. He was often called "The Gene Debs of Dixie," "The Norman Thomas with a Southern Accent" and sometimes even "The Saint of the STFU." Howard Kester's life is an inspiration to all who believe in racial and social justice.

Left: *STFU initiation, 1937. W. L. Blackstone administers oath to the man with his hands tied, a ritual borrowed from fraternal orders, and symbolizing that the union is the strongest of all ties. Rev. Blackstone became the STFU representative on the President's Committee on Farm Tenancy in 1937.* Above: *George Stith, 19-year-old sharecropper of Cotton Plant, Arkansas, borrowed a dime to pay dues to join the STFU. He is still active in the struggle today.*

A Report "Too Hot to Print"

Mary Connor Myers, the investigator for the Secretary of Agriculture, arrived the day that Ward Rodgers was given a preliminary court hearing. The striking figure of the red-haired woman lawyer was in marked contrast to the circus atmosphere of the makeshift courtroom in a vacant store building.

In a few weeks Mrs Myers gathered evidence from hundreds of sharecroppers who had been denied government subsidy payments for plowing up their cotton crop and had been evicted from their homes. Often Mrs Myers would rent a car and hire a driver.

One cold January day I was asked to drive her to the Twist plantation, and to help find a number of men who had made complaints to the USDA office in Washington. We worked late, interviewing and writing out sworn statements for each man. The train for Memphis had left, so I drove the government investigator there.

Before we reached Memphis, the roads were covered with sleet and ice. Mrs Myers insisted that her driver spend the night at the Peabody Hotel, where she had rooms. The Peabody was then the center of activity for all of the delta plantation coun-

Howard Kester, "The Gene Debs of Dixie"

try. In those days it was said that the Mississippi River delta started in the lobby of the Peabody Hotel, and ended in Catfish Row in Vicksburg. Though I was nearly thirty years of age, I had never before spent a night in a hotel, or experienced the luxury of a hot bath in a real bathtub.

When Myers returned to Washington, her report was suppressed by an assistant to Henry Wallace, who reported that "It was too hot to print." Though never made public, and removed from the official records of the U.S. Department of Agriculture, a member of Congress read it and reported that Mrs Myers substantiated the charges made by the union. The Secretary of Agriculture refused to allow his legal section to enter into the sharecroppers' suit seeking justice under the law.

The Man Led Around on a Leash by an Underdog

Inside the Department of Agriculture, a storm was brewing, caused by the suppression of the Mary Connor Myers report. Three officials were fired for demanding release of the report—among them, Gardner Jackson. The son of a well-to-do Colorado banker and mine-owner, Jackson, when a news reporter on the Boston *Globe*, broke the Sacco-Vanzetti case, convinced that the two anarchist leaders were guilty only of radical beliefs. Jackson became the Secretary of the Defense Committee that carried on an unsuccessful campaign throughout the world to save these two gentle men from execution.

My first introduction to "Pat" Jackson occurred when nine of us, members of the STFU, were picketing the U.S. Department of Agriculture one day in March of 1935. I was called to by Mrs Myers, and

stopped picketing to speak with her. A policeman threatened to jail me if I didn't keep moving with the line. Then there were calls from the huge crowd of onlookers, asking that the famed singer, A. B. Brookins, give the union song. The picketline stopped, and the union men began singing "We Shall Not Be Moved." The same policeman yelled, "Old man, if you don't stop that singing, I'll run you in." Out of the crowd came a man with a commanding presence, and a booming voice, demanding of the policeman, "By what right do you interfere with this man and his friends?" Said the policeman, "He is violating the District Ordinance against singing on the street." Jackson's reply was scorching. "You know very well there is no such law in the District of Columbia." The onlookers surged forward, and the policeman hurriedly left the scene to Jackson. The Washington *Post* carried a front-page picture of the STFU pickets and an editorial, comparing the nine sharecroppers, victims of the New Deal in Agriculture, with 3000 County Agents also in Washington at the time to sing the praises of the New Deal in Agriculture.

This was the beginning of Jackson's lifelong friendship and service to the Southern Tenant Farmers' Union and its successor organizations, lasting until the day he died in 1968. Jackson was also the unpaid representative of all the underdogs in American life. Among them were the American Indians, the nation's farm workers, black people and the Hispanics. Wherever there was injustice, Gardner "Pat" Jackson would be found fighting the battle of the underdog.

Gardner "Pat" Jackson, volunteer lobbyist for the STFU from 1935 to 1968. "Pat" also spoke for all the underdogs in the USA.

Night Riders on the Prowl, and STFU Membership on the Rise

A pastor of one of the largest churches in the area was asked by a New York *Times* reporter if the activities of the opposition to the STFU stemmed from the Ku Klux Klan. ''No,'' replied the Rev. J. Abner Sage, ''the Klan has such a bad reputation, that we decided to just call ourselves 'The Night Riders'.'' The Night Riders prowled the highways. I moved my family to safety in Memphis. Meetings were broken up, churches were burned. Homes of union members were machinegunned. Two men were killed. The home of the union's lawyer, Mr Carpenter, was fired into by the Night Riders. The union was driven underground, and I traveled the back country roads I knew well, dodging the Night Riders.

Mistakenly believing that the union had been destroyed, the larger cotton planters announced that the wage for picking cotton would be reduced from 60 cents paid the year before to 40 cents per hundred pounds (or from $1.25 per day to 80 cents.) The union responded at the height of the cotton picking season by calling a stay-at-home strike for $1.00 per hundred (about $2.00 a day). The union members had agreed that when the rate reached 75 cents they would all return to work. Cotton hung in the bolls. An investigator of the Arkansas Labor Department reported that he traveled over three counties where the strike centered and found only five people at work in the fields. The strike was won, and more than 25,000 new members joined the union.

Above: *Melvin Swinea, STFU Volunteer Organizer, Forrest City, Arkansas, 1937.* (Photo by Louise Boyle) Left: *Photo of actual wrappers on sticks of dynamite thrown into churchyard, February 21, 1936. The dynamite landed in soft mud and failed to explode.* (Photo by Howard Kester)

Above: *Evicted for joining the STFU.* Far right: *Norman Thomas of the Socialist Party visits evicted sharecroppers from the Dibble Plantation near Parkin, Arkansas, early 1936.* Right: *Evelyn Smith came to work for the STFU for a month and stayed for four years.*

Women Activists in the STFU

Taking part in all of the union activities, from the day she arrived in Memphis from New Orleans to become the union's first office secretary, was a dynamic young woman. Evelyn Smith had heard Norman Thomas tell about the plight of the Arkansas sharecroppper. She accepted a job at the union office for the sum of $10 a month. Instead of the one month she had agreed to work, she remained for four years in the thick of everything that happened. Evelyn sparked the first Women's Liberation Movement within the union. She helped the women attain full status in the union, and they soon became the driving force in the organization. She was with Howard Kester when he and the union lawyer were nearly lynched, following the breaking up of a union meeting of blacks and whites, where people were beaten as they jumped out of windows to escape.

Evelyn rode the back country roads with me, contacting union members at night, dodging the Night Riders on the prowl. She and another woman found the stockade where thirteen union members were being held in slavery. (This was the first evidence that led to the conviction of plantation-owner and deputy-sheriff Paul D. Peacher, on charges of peonage.) Whether on a trip into Arkansas, or with a delegation of sharecroppers to Washington, Evelyn was ready to go upon a few minutes' notice.

With Howard Kester, Evelyn co-authored the colorful "Ceremony of the Land," which became part of the program at all the union's conventions.

Over the years many women—Carrie Dilworth, Myrtle Lawrence, Henrietta McGhee, Deacy Real, Alberta Hynds Richburg and others mentioned elsewhere in these pages—took an active and important part in the struggles of the STFU.

STFU leader Myrtle Lawrence, author of the song, "Down in old St. Francis County, many a poor tenant has lost his home, and me, oh God, I am one." Mrs Lawrence, shown here in a 1937 photo, regularly asked for the Union's most dangerous assignments. (Photo by Louise Boyle)

Above: *Paul D. Peacher, Deputy Sheriff and Marshall of Earle, Arkansas, 1935-36, who arrested and jailed 13 STFU members and sentenced them to work on his own plantation, holding them in his stockade until the Union got the FBI to investigate. He was convicted of peonage in U.S. Court, 1936.* Right: *This emblem designed by Rockwell Kent for the "End Peonage in Arkansas" campaign in 1936, was circulated by the Workers' Defense League, and created quite a stir. The ensuing conviction of Deputy Sheriff and plantation-owner Peacher was hailed by sharecroppers and field workers as a great victory.*

The Strike of '36 and the Songs of John Handcox

In 1936 the union tried again—this time seeking $1.50 for a ten-hour day, and a union contract. On May 18 the union called a great big strike.

It was at this time that John L. Handcox, the black sharecropper-organizer and troubadour of the Southern Tenant Farmers' Union, started composing and singing his songs. The most famous of all is "Roll the Union On." Among America's labor songs, this ranks third, following "Solidarity Forever," written by Ralph Chaplin of the Industrial Workers of the World (IWW), and "We Shall Not Be Moved," first sung by the West Virginia miners in their 1929 strike, but later adopted as the official song of the STFU.

John Handcox's first composition was written on ruled tablet paper and handed to me with the request, "Mitch, I got a piece I want you to put in our paper." "The Sharecropper and the Planter" began with

> When a sharecropper dies,
> He is buried in a box,
> Without any necktie
> And without any socks.

Handcox wrote many songs and poems, most of which were recorded, and are today in the Folk Song Collection at the Library of Congress. Among these is "Mean Things Happening in This Land."

The union had trouble in 1936. It was a dry spring. The rain didn't fall, grass and weeds did not grow, and there was less need for hoe-hands to chop the cotton. Spontaneously, union members began marches through the plantations. (See partial transcript of the *March of Time* film.) The Governor of Arkansas sent in the National Guard to break the strike. John Hand-

cox sang, "I don't want to be like Governor Futrell in my heart." The planters retaliated. The marchers were attacked as the long lines moved down the plantation roads, calling out any workers still in the fields.

Jim Reese, white, and Frank Weems, black, were in the lead in a march near Earle, Arkansas. Both were beaten to the ground and left for dead. Eliza Nolden was so badly injured that she died. Frank Weems' body disappeared. The union folks were sure he had been killed. A white minister, the Rev. Claude Williams of Little Rock, and a white woman, Willie Sue Blagden, member of a prominent Memphis family, went to investigate. They were caught by planters and beaten with leather harness straps. In the August 1936 *March of Time* these scenes were reenacted. The *Time-Life* production was shown in over 6,000 movie theaters. Newspapers all over the country ran front-page stories. "Minister and Woman Flogged," read a headline in the *New York World-Telegram*. It was only a matter of weeks after pictures of Miss Blagden's bruised thighs were shown until Pres. Roosevelt appointed a Committee on Farm Tenancy.

The union learned of a peonage camp where thirteen workers were being held under guard on the plantation of Deputy Sheriff Paul D. Peacher. The FBI investigated the union's charges, and Peacher was indicted and convicted in federal court of holding men in slavery. Peacher had led the Night Riders in breaking up meetings, burning churches and schoolhouses, and shooting into homes of union people.

Once the outer guards warned a group of people holding a union meeting that the Night Riders were coming. They all ran into the woods to hide. In their hurry, the lamp was left burning. Peacher, heading his band, kicked in the door and was silhouetted in the light. A white union man, with his high-powered rifle trained on the door, was about to shoot Peacher

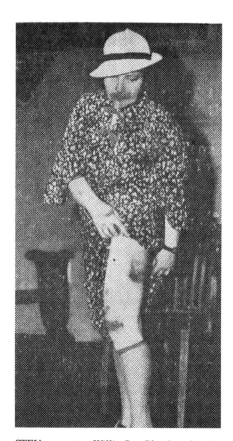

STFU supporter Willie Sue Blagden showing bruises received from flogging, Arkansas, 1936. This photo was reproduced coast-to-coast in American newspapers. Soon afterward Roosevelt appointed a Committee on Farm Tenancy.

when his black partner, hidden by his side, touched him and said, "Brother, don't shoot. The union is going to take care of Mr. Peacher." And the union did. The backbone of Arkansas terror was broken.

STFU Organizer John L. Handcox, farm labor's troubadour in the 1930s, composed many songs based on spirituals, of which "Roll the Union On" is the best known. The title of another of his songs, "Mean Things Happening in This Land," later became the title of H. L. Mitchell's full-length biography of this movement. (Photo by Evelyn Smith Munro)

Attempts to Assassinate H. L. Mitchell Foiled

In addition to narrow escapes at night on the back roads, there were attempts to assassinate me in broad daylight. Once when I was speaking at an open-air meeting, a young sharecropper—a follower of J. O. Green, leader of Nazi-like rivals who wanted to segregate black and white sharecroppers and who used a hooked cross as their emblem—attempted to shoot me in the back. An elderly union man grabbed the gun in Duffy's hand and the bullet struck the floor behind me. Thinking it was a firecracker thrown by a planter's stooge, I kept on talking. It was afterward learned that Duffy had been promised a team of mules and a 40-acre farm if he would kill me.

After the strike was over, I stopped one afternoon at Commonwealth College, the little labor college in the mountains of western Arkansas, along with Tony Peterson, my self-appointed bodyguard. We were en route to an STFU Executive Committee Meeting at Muskogee, Oklahoma.

Several members of our union were at Commonwealth, among them Walter and Myrtle Moskop. At the January Convention, Myrtle had been elected a member of the Committee, replacing her husband. I called on the Moskops, along with the Director of the College. Without warning, Moskop attempted to kill me, emptying a pistol at me within ten feet, but missing his target. Wresting the pistol away from Walter, Myrtle called, "Run, Mitch! He has a shotgun in the back room, and he will kill you sure." Down the mountainside ran the college director, and I was right behind him yelling, "Tony! Tony! Come quick! Moskop's trying to kill me!" These incidents were never reported to the authorities. There were no charges brought, no arrests made. Workingclass justice prevailed.

The Revolt Spreads

Oklahoma!

The only armed revolt against the U.S. government in this century occurred in 1917, when the tenant farmers of southeast Oklahoma, near Durant and Shawnee, started a march to take over the state capitol in Oklahoma City. They were members of an anti-war movement called "The Working Class Union." The idea was that the farmers and workers would revolt and take over the state, and then the federal government in Washington, and end World War I. Members of the Working Class Union started driving a small herd of cattle before them. Since it was summertime and the corn was green, they proposed to make their meals of roast beef and roasting ears. The governor called out the state militia, broke up the march, jailed the leaders and instituted a reign of terror throughout the state.

Up to this point, Oklahoma had had the strongest socialist movement of any state, with over 50,000 members. Eugene Debs polled 30% of the Oklahoma vote in 1912. The Socialist Party was strong among the miners in the state, and even stronger among the tenant farmers. The Oklahoma Renters Union had been formed earlier. Many of its members were left-wing socialists and some also belonged to the Industrial Workers of the World, or Wobblies. The flamboyant leader of one of the groups was Tad Cumbie, who wore a red shirt, and called himself "The Gray Horse of the Prairies" and the Commander-in-Chief of the Green Corn Rebellion.

There is evidence that the Working Class Union and similar secret societies were active throughout Oklahoma, and that they were as strong among the wheat farmers in the western half of the state as among the cotton tenant farmers in the southeast. J. R. Butler, STFU President from 1935 to 1942, was a member of the Working Class Union in White County, Arkansas, but had known nothing of the rebellion in Oklahoma until it was smashed by the authorities.

A meeting of the democratically elected Council on the Delta Cooperative Farm. This Council made all decisions regarding operation of the farm. (Photo by A. Hacker)

The Delta Cooperative Farm, near Clarksdale, Mississippi. Founded as a place of refuge for evicted sharecroppers from the Dibble Plantation near Parkin, Arkansas, it soon expanded to Providence Cooperative Farms in Holmes County. It ceased to function after attacks by the White Citizens Council put the farm's manager and doctor on trial for their "strange racial views."

Opposition to America's entry into World War I had been widespread, especially among socialists, although many Democrats also felt betrayed by Woodrow Wilson, who was elected in 1916 on the platform, "He Kept Us Out of War." In any event, with the suppression of the Green Corn Rebellion, the nation's strongest socialist movement was broken, and voted to dissolve. Remnants of the old Renters Union, however, still existed as late as the mid-1930s.

Odis L. Sweeden, Volunteer Organizer

One fine morning early in 1935, Odis L. Sweeden, sitting in his outhouse in Muskogee, read about the Southern Tenant Farmers' Union in the *American Guardian*, a paper edited by Socialist Party organizer Oscar Ameringer in Oklahoma City. Sweeden wrote to me at Box 207, Tyronza, Arkansas, and offered his services as a volunteer in Oklahoma.

Odis L. Sweeden was a member of the Cherokee Indian Nation and had been engaged in organizing WPA workers and other unemployed, many of them tenants on cotton farms owned by banks, insurance companies and individual absentee landlords. On March 12, 1935, an STFU local was formed near Muskogee, and within a year, seventy-five more units were formed in the state, totaling some 8,500 members. As STFU Secretary, I soon paid a visit to the outposts of the union in Texas and Oklahoma.

In Oklahoma I met with the Choctaw Tribal Council; trilingual Sweeden acted as interpreter. Since most of the members of that tribe were tenant farmers, I urged them to join the STFU. The Tribal Council gave me a respectful hearing, and then the Chief arose and replied ceremoniously in Choctaw. I thought I had made a real hit, but then Sweeden told me what the Chief had said:

The white man talks well. Our brother from Muskogee talks well. But Choctaws don't need organizing. We are already organized. When the white man and the black man are ready to take back the land, just let us know, and we shall get our guns and come, too.

Tenants and small farmers who were members of the Creek Tribe, near Okmulgee, had already joined the STFU. I visited the home of John Berryhill, whose father was Captain J. H. Berryhill, of the Creek Indian Nation's Dragoons—the troops that had conducted the last execution under tribal law, on the grounds of the Creek Council House, which I also visited. The convicted murderer had been allowed to harvest his final crop before coming in unescorted to be executed.

Throughout the next two years Odis L. Sweeden remained an organizer for the STFU, and was also elected a Vice-President. He conducted a campaign for tenants, sharecroppers and farm laborers in southeast Oklahoma. When Governor Marlin appointed a special committee on farm tenancy, Sweeden was named as one of its members.

Sweeden followed his members on their migration to the far west, to escape the dust-storms, after being blown out or tractored out in their native state. He returned to Muskogee in 1939, just in time to get embroiled in the union's battles with the Communist-dominated United Cannery, Agricultural, Packing and Allied Workers of America. Offered a job by the CIO chief, Donald Henderson, Sweeden abandoned his first choice—the STFU.

One day early in 1940, en route to Oklahoma City, I stopped at the New Huber Hotel in Muskogee. I asked the bellman if he had seen Odis Sweeden recently. ''Yes,'' he said, ''about a year ago Mr Sweeden stopped by to see that little black-haired man

Union people meet for a fish fry on the Twist Cooperative Farm Project.

from New York. Went up to his room. We heard the damnedest racket, and the desk clerk said for me to go up and see what was going on.'' Rushing upstairs, he heard more noise, opened the door, and ''there was Mr Sweeden and that man from New York, slugging away at each other.'' The bellman said he shouted for them to stop, as they were damaging hotel property, ''and Mr Sweeden picked up the piss-pot and jammed it over the man's head. It got stuck, and we had a time getting it off over the man's scratched-up face.''

Sixteen families were evicted from homes on the C. H. Dibble Plantation, January 16, 1936.

Visiting Sweeden the next day, he told me, "I had to work out on Don. *He had lied to me.*" When I returned to STFU headquarters I told this story to the STFU Executive Council, which restored Sweeden as a member and officer of that body.

Sweeden claimed that he was a cousin of Pretty Boy Floyd, the notorious outlaw, and that he sometimes met the "Robin Hood of the Oklahoma Hills" when he was hiding out between bank robberies. Edwin Lanham's 1939 novel, *The Stricklands*, about an Oklahoma STFU organizer whose brother was an outlaw, is unmistakably a fictionalized story of Odis L. Sweeden.

The last I heard of Sweeden he was working as a railway clerk in San Antonio, Texas, in 1948. He may still be alive even today. If so, he is most likely still raising hell, as he did fifty years ago.

Farm Security Created by Congress

I made my first plane trip, an all-night ride to Philadelphia, to attend the Democratic Convention of 1936. There I met and confronted Senator Joe T. Robinson of Arkansas, Majority Leader of the U.S. Senate, about representation of the STFU on the President's Committee on Farm Tenancy, which had a member from every farm group except the one it purported to study.

This bit of politicking resulted in the foundation of what became the Farm Security Administration. A union member and cotton-patch preacher, Rev. William L. Blackstone, was appointed to the Committee. After holding public hearings throughout the country, the President's Committee recommended that loans be made to a few landless farmers to purchase farms of their own. The union then filed a mi-

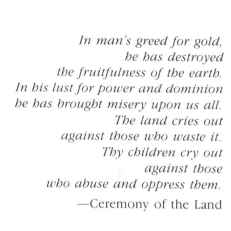

In man's greed for gold,
he has destroyed
the fruitfulness of the earth.
In his lust for power and dominion
he has brought misery upon us all.
The land cries out
against those who waste it.
Thy children cry out
against those
who abuse and oppress them.

—Ceremony of the Land

nority report to the President's Committee on Farm Tenancy, recommending that an agency be created to make rural rehabilitation loans, to continue experiments in cooperative farming, to build housing for farm families, to extend the minimum wage, to guarantee farm workers the right to organize and to bargain collectively, as well as to include farmers and farm workers under other recently enacted social welfare legislation. The first and only rural poverty program of all time in America came from the President's Committee on Farm Tenancy—"Studies of Farm Problems." The Farm Security Administration was created to undo some of the evils of the New Deal in Agriculture.

The CIO in the Cottonfields

In 1937, the CIO and John L. Lewis agreed to set up an international union for agricultural and can-

nery workers. This was part of a plan by Harry Bridges, the Longshoreman Union leader, to organize all workers in California on farms and in food-processing. Mr Bridges termed this a march inland by the CIO from the sea. But Donald Henderson, a former tutor at Columbia University, and then a member of the Central Committee of the Communist Party, was slated to head the new CIO union. The founding convention met in Denver, and while the STFU had more members than all the other unions in attendance put together, there were only nine delegates there to represent the sharecroppers.

Soon after the Convention got under way, Henderson called me aside and proposed that he would get me elected to the number two spot in the new CIO affiliate, provided that I would join the Communist Party and accept its discipline. This I indignantly refused to do, saying that many of my friends were

New Dealers, and that I was a member of the Socialist Party headed by Norman Thomas. Henderson tried to persuade me, saying I could be a secret member of the Communist Party. I said I would not take the job of Secretary-Treasurer under such circumstances, and that if I were going to join the Communist Party, I would announce it to the newspapers, and would never keep it a secret. Henderson then asked me if I thought J. R. Butler would agree to become Vice-President. I replied, "If you make him the same proposition as you have made to me, that Arkansas hillbilly will beat hell out of you."

The Strange Case of Claude C. Williams

An amazing document was found by the STFU President at his home in Memphis. It was addressed to the Central Committee of the Communist Party USA. It read as follows:

A situation has now arisen which offers an extraordinary opportunity to move into the most important organization in the agricultural South. H. L. Mitchell, who has always opposed the Party, is away on leave. J. R. Butler, who is friendly to our line, is in charge.

The writer went on to ask that the Central Committee provide $500 to take over the Southern Tenant Farmers' Union. The paper had been left accidentally by Claude C. Williams, who had been beaten by planters in Arkansas following the 1936 strike of cotton choppers. Notations on the paper were in the handwriting of Williams. I was away on an assignment with a New Deal agency, the National Youth Administration, and read the news of the attempt by the CP to take over the STFU in a South Carolina newspaper. This was the beginning of the inter-union conflict that threatened to disrupt the movement that

F. R. Betton of Cotton Plant, Arkansas, STFU Vice-President from 1938 to 1970.

the planters had been unable to destroy with Klanlike night-riders, beatings, jailings, burning of churches and meeting-places, and killing its members.

The Missouri Roadside Demonstration of 1939

The most spectacular event to occur in the sharecropper movement came in January of 1939 when 1700 black and white families moved out on the public highways and sat down in protest against being evicted from their cabins in the cottonfields. Led by a charismatic black minister, Owen H. Whitfield, this movement attracted widespread attention in the press and newsreels.The basic reason for the evictions was that the STFU had at last secured an order requiring that government subsidy checks be sent direct to sharecroppers and tenants for their proper share of the money being paid for not planting cotton. The Missouri planters offered the tenants a choice— become wage-laborers or get off the plantation. This change in status was unacceptable to the sharecroppers, and the blacks and whites alike determined, at a union meeting in a Negro church, to move out and camp alongside the highway and watch the world go by. At the meeting they sang:

> *Homeless, homeless are we*
> *Just as homeless as homeless can be.*
> *We don't get nothing for our labor,*
> *So homeless, homeless are we.*

Thad Snow, a sympathetic landowner who attended the meeting, described it: "The churchyard was jammed full of old cars, It was exciting. I wouldn't have missed it on a bet. We expected Whitfield to gravely exhort his people to be steadfast. To try to bolster up their courage for the danger and hardships ahead. But Whitfield went to the pulpit, and spoke:

Above: *Evicted sharecroppers camp, U.S. Highway 61, south of Sikeston, Missouri, January 1939.* Left: *State Police break up the evicted sharecroppers' roadside demonstration, January 20, 1939.* (Photo by Arthur Rothstein)

"Here our possessions lie." STFU evicted sharecroppers' roadside demonstration, January 1939. (Photo by Arthur Rothstein)

The Hebrew children had to leave someplace, had to get to someplace better. [That's right!] When they went they couldn't go back. And old Boss Pharaoh and his riding bosses in their shiny chariots couldn't catch 'em. [No!] Couldn't catch 'em then, ain't gonna stop us now! [Amen!] 'Cause the time is come we too must make an exodus. [Cheers.] Would you rather starve to death, like an old hound wandering from door to door, or make a stand? [Make a stand!] Then, if we're gonna starve, let's starve right out on the highway so the whole world can see! [The entire crowd leaped to its feet!]

"It's a shame that a recording was not made of Whit's speech. For that matter, a recording of the Sermon on the Mount ought to have been made. In a way, the two occasions were comparable."

Mitchell at the White House

While Owen Whitfield was calling on the Lord, I called on Mrs Roosevelt at the White House in Washington. When the sharecroppers evicted from plantations in Missouri moved out on the highways of southeast Missouri in protest, I had been in New York City fundraising, and had seen, in the New York

Times, pictures of people I knew camped out in the bitter cold, with old people and children huddled around campfires. While STFU officers in Memphis headed for Missouri, I went to Washington to seek help. Our friends in the New Deal said that the protesters would freeze and starve before the wheels of government could be set in motion to save them. Mr Delano, chairman of the American Red Cross, advised me that the Red Cross could do nothing to alleviate a ''man-made'' disaster. Aubrey Williams arranged an appointment for me to see Mrs Roosevelt, who agreed to meet me at six o'clock at the White House.

Just before the appointed time, I drove through the open gates in a taxicab that stopped at the entrance where today only important visitors enter and are met by the President. I paid my taxi fare of twenty-five cents, including tip, and was met by the chief usher, a middle-aged black man, who escorted me into a big red room. The room had been cleared for an official reception to be held that evening. There was only a single chair and a sofa. I sat in first one and then the other. Intimidated by the place where Thomas Jefferson, Abraham Lincoln and other great people had once lived, I afterward said that if I had known how to leave the President's home, I would have done so. Instead, I waited for Mrs Roosevelt to arrive. Thirty minutes later she rushed in, breathless, apologizing for keeping me waiting.

I had seen Mrs Roosevelt in pictures and newsreels, and had thought her features and high-pitched voice unattractive, but here she was, one of the most beautiful women I had ever seen.

Eleanor Roosevelt was in her early fifties, trim and stately, and most impressive. I was immediately put at ease as she said to me, ''Sit down, tell me all about it, and what I can do to help those poor people

camped on the highway in the snow.'' I asked if she would persuade the President to have the National Guard send tents and field kitchens to shelter and feed them. Mrs Roosevelt said she would place a memorandum on the President's bedside table, so it would be the first thing he would read that evening, and that she would talk to him the following morning and see that he did something about it.

She then said, ''I intend to write about the Missouri situation in 'My Day' [a column published in many newspapers]. What shall I ask my readers to do?'' While that had not been on the agenda, I rose to the occasion and suggested that she ask everyone to send food, clothing and money to help care for the people who were in need. Mrs Roosevelt promised to do so. Thereafter, whenever Mrs Roosevelt chanced to meet me, she would greet me as ''the young man from Missouri.''

The President did instruct the Governor of Missouri to mobilize a unit of the National Guard, which was

This letter from Jasmine Nielsen is one of many received from youngsters of the Leal Grammar School in Urbana, Illinois, after H. L. Mitchell spoke to them in April 1985. This is Jasmine's picture of Mitchell nervously waiting in the Red Room at the White House, and the sudden appearance of the stately First Lady.

49

Prefiguring the Civil Rights movement of the 1960s, 1500 men, women and children sat down on the U.S. highways in the bootheel of Missouri in early January of 1939. Within a year, the federal government built nearly 600 homes for the homeless in a project proposed by the STFU and known as the Delmo Farm Labor Homes. In 1945, when these homes were about to be sold, the STFU again aroused the nation and the homes were sold to the people who lived in them. Shown here is a typical Delmo Farm Labor Home, still owned and occupied by the original campers from 1939.

The Delmo Farm Labor Homes were bought by residents at $800 each. Payments of $10.20 per month began in January 1948; all payments were completed in 1954.

50

prepared for dispatch to the scene of the encampment. The planters of Southeast Missouri learned about the order, and pressured the State Health Department to declare the evicted sharecropper roadcamps a menace to public health. State Highway Patrolmen moved in and loaded the families and their possessions onto wagons and trucks and dumped them on back country roads, where they were out of sight. One group, mainly blacks, were set out in the open air on the New Madrid Spillway, between the levee and Mississippi River, and held there under guard by local deputies, without drinking water or food for several days. They were rescued after two messengers from the camp escaped to St. Louis and contacted union supporters there. Food, clothing and money came in to the collection point in Arkansas, and we mobilized union organizers and dispatched them to Missouri. Usually a white man and a black man made up a team. They searched the back roads bringing relief to the needy. Soon the machinery of government began to move. Small grants were given to all who applied. The union saw to it that those in need met the government agents and received the help available.

Soon, I was back in Washington with a delegation from Missouri. We proposed the development of a cooperative farming community with housing, community facilities and land enough to provide subsistence food until there were jobs available in the cottonfields in the spring and fall. Ten communities were selected, and 50 to 100 homes were built in each place, to a total of 595 houses. Families who were on the roadside moved into the government houses, and were required to pay only a small sum in rent.

Near the end of World War II, Congress ordered all community-type farm or housing projects operated for workers by the Farm Security Administration to be sold to the highest bidder, dismantled and moved off land owned by the federal government. This marked the beginning of what later became known as McCarthyism (after U.S. Senator Joe McCarthy of Wisconsin), when far-rightism in the United States raised its slimy head. The poor were its first victims. Since there was an organization of workers in Southeastern Missouri, the Delmo Labor Homes were saved from destruction. Learning of the impending sale of the homes and the removal of the people's possessions, we started mobilizing help in the fields and in Washington and elsewhere. A young minister, David S. Burgess, assigned to work with the union, was placed in charge. Burgess raised $87,000. A housing corporation was formed and bought 550 homes, and sold them on long terms at low interest rates to the residents. Members of Congress who were friends of the STFU blocked action while funds were raised.

The Delmo Labor Homes are still occupied today, many of them by descendants of those families camped alongside the highways in the winter of '39.

Farm Labor in Wartime

Not all of the problems of the sharecroppers and farm workers were solved while the Farm Security Administration continued from 1938 to the mid-1940s. There were other programs that helped, but did not end poverty in the rural south.

Soon after Pearl Harbor, the big farmers decided that the best way to maintain an over-supply of workers for jobs on farms was to bring workers into the United States from Mexico and the from Caribbean Islands such as the Bahamas and Jamaica.

The STFU protested, and demanded that the War Manpower Commission provide jobs for unemployed

STFU Organizer Carrie Dilworth, a lifelong labor and civil rights activist, as she appeared in the 1930s. In the '60s her home served as headquarters of the Student Non-Violent Coordinating Committee in Arkansas, and was burned to the ground by the KKK.

and underemployed American farm workers in the South.

The FSA agreed to provide transportation for 2,000 union workers and their families to go to New Mexico, Arizona and Texas to harvest a special crop of "pima" cotton that the army claimed was needed to replace silk from China formerly used in observation- and barrage-balloons. (All imports from China had been cut off by the Japanese Imperial Armed Forces sweeping through Asia.) Residents of the Delmo Labor Homes were the first to go.

Then Congress, pressured by the big farm organizations—who feared that the union would organize farm labor—enacted a law authorizing the importation of Mexican Nationals. The act prohibited the use of government funds for recruiting and transporting any domestic agricultural worker, unless each individual had the written consent of his county extension service agent to accept such a job away from his home county.

Then, in cooperation with Leon B. Schachter, head of local union 56 of the Amalgamated Meat Cutters in New Jersey, we worked out an organized migration plan whereby workers in the south recruited by the STFU were sent by train, bus or plane to fill jobs in food-processing and on farms where the New Jersey union had contracts and/or contacts. Under the organized migration plan, over 12,000 men and women farmworkers were placed on jobs during wartime.

Farm Labor Under the AFL Umbrella, and Washington's Smallest Lobby

Soon after World War II ended, the STFU began seeking entry into the official labor movement. Realizing that reaction was on its way (the notorious Taft-Hartley "slave labor act" was passed in 1947), and that our small independent organization would inevitably be smashed by the government, we mobil-

Left: *En route from Arkansas.* Above: *Their first plane ride. Transported to New Jersey, college women join STFU to work in food-processing plant at Seabrook Farms during World War II.*

California, here we are.

ized our friends in and out of the labor movement and the government. Due to the fact that the remnants of the Cannery and Agricultural Union were still in the CIO, there was little hope of finding a home within that organization, eventually to be headed by Walter P. Reuther. Instead, we enlisted the help of the Meat Cutters, long-standing members of the AFL. Together, we maneuvered the entry of the STFU, now renamed National Farm Labor Union—of which I was President—into the AFL. So the movement survived until 1960. Neither Richard Nixon, Joe McCarthy, nor any of the other reactionaries of the 1940s and '50s were able to smash completely the farm labor movement.

In 1948, the headquarters of the National Farm Labor Union were moved to the nation's capital. There, for twelve years my second wife Dorothy and I operated a two-person lobby for farmworkers, with the help of many others. I served on the Federal Advisory Council of the U.S. Department of Labor for ten years, and used it as a sounding-board for the nation's farmworkers. While in Washington, we secured the extension of Social Security to farmworkers and farmers, from which they were previously excluded. The foundation was laid for extension of minimum wage to farmworkers in the 1960s. We fought for the extension of the National Labor Relations Act to agriculture, but farmworkers remained—and still remain—excluded from this social welfare legislation.

The Di Giorgio Strike

Soon after the National Farm Labor Union became an affiliate of the AFL, I was asked by the California Federation of Labor to organize the workers on the corporation farms and ranches of the state. I persuaded Hank Hasiwar, a veteran of the war in the Pacific, to become the West Coast organizer for the National Farm Labor Union. Hasiwar set about organizing California agriculture as if it were an automobile factory. There were several preliminary battles, of which some were won and some were lost. Then the workers were organized on the Di Giorgio Fruit Corporation with 18,000 acres, a packinghouse, and the world's largest winery, all located near the farm worker towns of Arvin and Lamont, in Kern County. It was here that the scenes of the movie *The Grapes of Wrath*, based on the novel by John Steinbeck, were filmed.

Out of 1,345 men and women employees, 1,100 joined the union, and when refused simple recognition, went on strike. The strike lasted over two years, and the picketlines stretching over twenty miles were some of the longest in labor history. The employer's weapon was the use of legally imported contract workers from Mexico. The NFLU with the help of AFL officials in Washington, persuaded the Secretary of State, General George Marshall, to withdraw the strikebreakers. The Corporation then began illegally importing workers from Mexico, and the Immigration Service joined the Union in conducting a hit-and-run guerrilla warfare against Di Giorgio, with raids on this illegal labor supply.

Di Giorgio retaliated by accusing the union of using "communistic" tactics. The California Senate Committee on Un-American Activities subpoenaed Hank Hasiwar and me to appear at a hearing in Los Angeles. The Chairman of the State Legislative Committee was one Jack Tenney, a member of the Musicians' Union, and prior to his anti-Red hunts noted solely for composing a hit song of the late 1940s called *Mexicali Rose*. In an obvious publicity ploy, Ten-

Migrant farmworkers. (Photo by Dorothea Lange)

Bust of Joseph DiGiorgio, Kern County, California.

ney put on the stand as his first witness the Secretary of the Los Angeles Communist Party, a painter named Frank Spector. He was a short, swarthy, longhaired man, looking like a caricature of a Communist. Tenney's first question, aimed at making the headlines of the Hearst-owned newspapers' first afternoon editions, was this: "Mr Spector, does the Communist Party support the Di Giorgio strike?" Replied Spector: "Of course we do, Jack. Don't you remember when you were a member of our faction, that we Communists support all strikes?" While Spector's actual words did not make the paper, the headline read: "Communist says Reds Support Di Giorgio Strike."

I was asked if Norman Thomas was not a Communist, and I replied that long before Tenney became a Communist-hunter, Norman Thomas was publicly opposing them. Hank Hasiwar was shown a letter he had received from me some weeks before. "Yes,"

said Hank, "how did you get that letter together? It was of no importance. I tore it up and threw it in the john in my hotel room." Chairman Tenney persisted: "But what does this mean, Mr. Hasiwar? 'Acerman is taking care of the John Reed angle?'" (John Reed was a famous American journalist who died in Russia during the Revolution of 1917, and whose body was buried in the wall of the Kremlin. In the 1930s there were organizations called "John Reed Clubs.") Jack Tenney was sure that he had nailed the National Farm Labor Union to the Communist cross. Hank, hesitating as if fearful of revealing the truth, replied: "John Reed is a labor recruiter in Texas who has been sending illegal aliens to California to work for Di Giorgio as strikebreakers in violation of federal law. Harry Acerman is Secretary of the Texas Federation of Labor, AFL, and he has gotten out a warrant for the arrest of that man John Reed." This hearing ended the attempt to pin the red label on the union. Richard

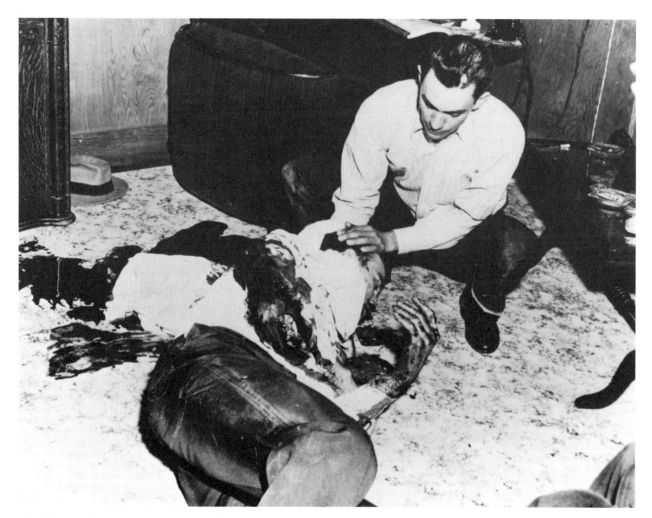

Left: *"Takes more than guns to kill an Okla-homan,"* said James G. Price of Marlow, Oklahoma after recovering from attempt to wipe out Kern County Farm Labor Union No. 218, Arvin, California, May 17, 1948. Above: James G. Price, President, Kern County Farm Labor Union No. 218.

M. Nixon, then a congressman, refused to sponsor an investigation by the House Un-American Activities Committee to crucify the NFLU after Tenney's fishing expedition had come to such a sorry end.

There was an attempt, however, by persons unknown, to wipe out the strike committee by gunfire. Hank Hasiwar was the intended victim of the assas-sination plot, but it was Jim Price, a local union leader, an Okie, who was struck by machinegun fire. Price almost bled to death before the union people could get him to the hospital in Bakersfield, 18 miles away. The only doctor in the area, D. D. Schmidt, company doctor for Di Giorgio, refused to give first-aid treatment, saying that he did not want to become involved.

Poverty in the Valley of Plenty:
A Labor Film Made with Reagan's Help

Soon after this outrage, Congresswoman Helen Gahagan Douglas brought to the strike scene a group of nationally known citizens. They were accompanied by the press, radio and newsreel crews, including CBS and NBC reporters. Through Mrs Douglas' influence, the Hollywood Film Council, composed of all the unions in the movie industry, agreed to make a thirty-minute documentary film titled *Poverty in the Valley of Plenty*. One of the people instrumental in raising the money and getting the film produced and distributed was none other than the President of the Screen Actors' Guild, Ronald Reagan. Reagan's union also made a donation of $5000 to the strike-fund of the Di Giorgio workers. In those days it was often said in AFL circles that Ronnie was so far over on Left that some believed he was cheating the Communist Party of its dues.

Ernesto Galarza, Man of Fire

The most unusual man ever in the American labor movement was Ernesto Galarza. A native of Mexico, his family came to the United States as refugees from the perils of the Mexican Revolution of 1910. They joined the stream of migrant workers, constantly on the move, harvesting the crops up and down the valleys of California. They lived alongside the irrigation ditch banks, where young Ernesto saw people dying of starvation and lack of sanitary facilities. As a boy of twelve years he pedaled a bicycle to Sacramento to contact state government officials about the plight of his people. An investigation was made, and relief given to the people. Ernesto was also advised to tell his people to organize a union. Some years were to intervene before Galarza got around to doing so.

Ernesto Galarza: A Scholar on the Ramparts

A bright young Mexican boy living in the barrios of Sacramento, Galarza made many friends. One was an old Wobbly who taught him why people such as he were victims of the system. Another was a woman of the oldest profession, who forbade him to enter her yard, but stacked empty bottles in the corner of it for him to retrieve and sell. Also, his teachers encouraged Ernesto in his quest for learning. One of the first Mexican labor immigrants to finish high school, he received a partial scholarship to Occidental College, supplemented with earnings from mowing lawns in nearby Pasadena. Later he got his Master's Degree from Stanford University, and finally his PhD in Anthropology from Columbia. Dr Ernesto Galarza was one of the first Mexican-Americans to attain such a status. Working mainly in the field of Foreign Relations, he became Chief of the Labor and Information Division of the Pan-American Union (now the Organization of American States). Galarza was later to tell the Foreign Relations Committee of the United States Senate that he resigned after becoming violently nauseated by the policies of the U.S. State Department in Latin America.

Ernesto Galarza came to the Washington Convention of the newly-chartered National Farm Labor Union, AFL (successor to the STFU) in 1947, to challenge that organization to organize the Spanish-speaking workers of the southwestern states. I persuaded him to become the union's Education and Research Director. Ernesto soon joined Hank Hasiwar in California, and there made his contribution to the Di Giorgio strike, and helped lead the cotton-pickers' strikes of 1949 and 1950. Singlehanded, in the late 1950s Galarza took on the battle with the power structure of the state and national governments. Training workers barely able to read and write, he exposed government agents in all their venality toward the nation's farm-workers. Writing and publishing book after book, Galarza documented the struggles of the various minorities, including the Okies in the fields. Becoming known as the "Scholar on the Ramparts," Ernesto Galarza was also termed the "John the Baptist" of his later counterpart, Cesar Chavez. During this period of his life of active union organizing, Galarza joined a delegation of U.S. trade unionists, at a joint conference in Mexico, and there challenged both groups to work out a program of organizing Mexican workers before they came to the United States as legal contract workers, or as illegals, known as "wetbacks." Following is an excerpt from an article published in the *Industrial Worker*, the IWW paper, published in Chicago:

Easily the most outstanding personality at the Conference was Ernesto Galarza, of the AFL Farm Workers. His faded khaki shirt open at the neck, he pleaded with the Mexican labor leaders for cooperation in an organizational drive. . . . [His appearance] contrasted sharply with the hand-painted ties of his bored and restless audience.

Mr Nixon Defends Corporation Farmers

The Di Giorgio Fruit Corporation demanded, and the union welcomed, an investigation of the Di Giorgio strike. I arranged to have the movie, *Poverty in the Valley of Plenty*, shown to the House Education and Labor Committee. The Chairman, John Lesinski of Michigan, appointed a subcommittee of three Democrats and two Republicans to make the investigation. Richard M. Nixon of California was on the subcommittee, and when the hearings were held in Bakersfield in November of 1949, the future President of the United States was there. Obviously defending the Di Giorgio Fruit Corporation, and

Ernesto Galarza on the picketline.

We covet no man's freedom,
no man's fields,
no man's houses or barns;
only our share
of the Eternal's earth.

—Ceremony of the Land

A few of the 1100 DiGiorgio strikers, members of the National Farm Labor Union (AFL) in California, 1947-1950.

acting as the prosecutor of the union witnesses, he tried to make each union man or woman who appeared as a witness into a criminal on trial for his or her life. He asked one union witness, "Where were you at seven o'clock on the night of November 31, 1948?" The union man replied, "I guess I was at home, that's about suppertime." Nixon attacked the straightforward Okie with, "Remember, you are under oath! You know very well there is no November 31st!" This exchange was edited out of the transcript of the record, but everyone present heard it.

Because of Nixon's mistreatment of union witnesses on the stand during this hearing, and a bitter exchange between Nixon and Hasiwar in a bar the previous evening, the union organizer was angry at the congressman. Then Nixon walked between Hasiwar and me and, placing his hands on our arms conspiratorially, said to us, "If you ever get into another hassle with these big growers here in California, and they accuse you of being Communists, you come to me. I'll straighten them out for you." Hasiwar, six-foot-three, towering over Nixon physically, drew back his fist, ready to hit him. I stopped him because it would never have done for a union organizer to strike a congressman, no matter how great the provocation.

Timed to coincide with the Bakersfield hearing was a lawsuit by the Di Giorgio Corporation, alleging that the movie, *Poverty in the Valley of Plenty*, contained libelous material. Named in the suit for $2,000,000 each were all the persons and organizations involved in making the movie. These included the American Federation of Labor, the California Federation of Labor, the Hollywood Film Council, the NFLU and its President and Chief Organizer. Most of the strikers had found other jobs, and not one ever went back to work for Di Giorgio. The labor organizations re-

fused to defend themselves against the lawsuit. The NFLU attorney, Alexander H. Schullman, offered to represent them all without a fee, but the powerful movie was withdrawn from circulation, though copies may still be in existence.

Hank Hasiwar in 1948.

American Federation of Labor caravan bringing food, clothing and financial aid to the Di Giorgio strikers.

The Okies' Last Stand

Early one morning the three remaining pickets on all-night duty at the gates of the Di Giorgio ranch were viciously attacked by ex-convicts hired by Di Giorgio to break the strike. Word spread quickly through the small farmworker towns, and more than a thousand men and women, all hastily armed with rifles, shotguns, pistols and clubs, assembled at the gates. They were all ready to march through and clean out Di Giorgio of strikebreakers, supervisors and all. The sheriff was there with a dozen heavily-armed deputies and several highway patrol cars were also on the scene.

The older unionists persuaded the younger ones to wait until Hank arrived at seven o'clock, as was his custom each day. When he got there, the men told him, "Hank, this is going to be it. We are going to settle this strike now." The thing that worried Hank most was that there were a number of older women who were always on the picketline, with clubs in hand, ready to lead the assault. Hank kept thinking these little old ladies were going to catch it first. The sheriff came to implore Hank to use his influence to quiet the mob of Okies. Hank told the sheriff that he was the man who had caused it all. "You know who beat these men nearly to death." One of the younger strikers walked up to the sheriff and said,

The union sent a delegation to meet with California Governor Earl Warren, who later became Chief Justice of the U. S. Supreme Court.

"John Lousalot, we are going to kill you first. We are going to shoot you dead." Hank knew that Johnny would be the first to go, and the sheriff's deputies would then likely kill Hank, and there would be a slaughter—-a big splash in the newspapers, many people dead and injured. The strike had been lost. The union had always opposed the use of violence. The older heads in the union crowd joined in persuading the people to disperse, and avoid killings.

The militant union members fanned out over the San Joaquin Valley working in the cotton fields. The cotton growers had reduced wages offered for picking cotton. With only two union organizers to lead them, 20,000 workers went on strike. They traversed the valley in jalopies, calling out the pickers still in the fields. A certain young cotton-picker was in the caravan each day, from the migrant camp at Corcoran. He was Cesar Chavez, who remembers getting his first union card from the National Farm Labor Union, AFL, and that H. L. Mitchell's signature was on the back of it.

The Hank Hasiwar Proviso

The union made its last major effort in the Imperial Valley in 1951. Nearly every field worker joined. There was support for the union effort among the merchants and other people in the small towns and

The strike force in the California Imperial Valley, 1951, composed mainly of Mexican-American farm-workers.

cities of the rich Imperial Valley. The union was determined to stop the use of Mexican nationals employed under contract, as well as the exploitation of illegal aliens known as ''wetbacks.'' Plans were carefully laid. Demands were made on the growers' association for recognition prior to the start of the melon harvest employing the largest number of Spanish-speaking residents during the winter months in the Imperial Valley. Local leadership had been developed and carefully trained.

The day came. All work ceased. Some of the employers sent trucks to old Mexico to bring in illegal aliens as strikebreakers. Hasiwar was awakened early one morning with the report that several trucks loaded with scabs were en route to the camps usually occupied by contract nationals. The sheriff and his men were waiting. Casey Zuniga, one of the local leaders of the Mexican-American community, was on the picketline, refusing to permit the trucks to enter the camp. As Casey Zuniga was threatening to shoot the driver if he moved his truck, Hank arrived. The sheriff demanded that he permit the trucks loaded with strikebreakers to enter the camp. Then Hank came up with a new idea: Why not make a citizen's arrest of the strikebreakers and escort them to the Border Patrol? This was done. Opposition to the use of scabs, not anti-Chicano sentiments, motivated the union's action. Every Spanish-speaking union member, often assisted by townspeople, got busy hauling in the strikebreakers.

One day the county sheriff called Hank to come down to the jail quick. Some woman had forty strikebreakers under citizen's arrest, and demanded that he jail them. The sheriff did not feel that the illegals were his responsibility, and besides he had no room in his jail.

In Washington, Willard Kelly, the Chief of the U.S. Border Patrol, called me, asking me as NFLU President to come in as soon as possible to the offices of the Immigration and Naturalization Service at the Department of Justice building. I found Kelly elated by the developments in the Imperial Valley. At last the conscientious Border Patrol Chief had found a way to enforce the law. Could I get the AFL and the CIO to instruct all of their members residing near the Mexico-U.S. border to make citizens' arrests of illegal aliens? The U.S. Border Patrol would put them across into old Mexico by the thousands. But union enforcement of the law was not to be. Congress quickly adopted a provision in the immigration statutes to prohibit the arrest of an illegal alien by anyone other than a uniformed Border Patrolman. This became known as the Hank Hasiwar Proviso.

On the march from Delano. Cesar Chavez welcomed en route.

The Secretary of Labor Makes a Deal

The union strike in the melon fields was also coming to an end. Representatives of twenty-seven of the largest growers in the Imperial Valley came to the union headquarters in El Centro, and promised to sign a union contract the next day, if the NFLU could stop the movement of legal contract-workers from Mexico. The growers were assured that the union could continue as they were doing, and keep both legal and illegal nationals out. I received word that the strike was ready to be settled, and that I should fly out to El Centro for a big celebration, a fiesta by the members of the Sindicato Agricola, Trabajadores Americanos (SANTA), as the Spanish-speaking Mexican-American workers called their union.

Unknown to union members and organizers in the Imperial, they had already become victims of a political deal. Edward A. Pauley, the millionaire oil bagman for the Democratic Party, had ridden a plane to Washington with Secretary of Labor Maurice Tobin. A deal had been made, and the Secretary certified the need for 7,000 contract workers to be brought in from Mexico. They were moved in during the night.

Cesar Chavez. (Photo by Cathy Murphy)

Union Defeated in Washington

Some days later I led a delegation to call on Maurice Tobin, Secretary of Labor. Attorney Joseph Rauh had papers ready to be filed in the U. S. District Court for an injunction against the Secretary of Labor. Maurice Tobin was combing his hair, rushing to the bathroom like he had dysentery. (There was evidently a telephone in his private bathroom.) The aged President of the AFL, William Green, was calling the President of NFLU, "Please, Brother Mitchell, don't

sue the Labor Department. That is organized labor's voice in government. It's our Department." My reply was, "Mr Green, if we can persuade Secretary Tobin to remove 7,000 Mexican nationals being used as strikebreakers out of the Imperial Valley, there will be no lawsuit."

Tobin was in direct contact by private telephone with both AFL headquarters and the melon-growers in California. Finally he came back to his seat and said, "Mr Rauh, Mr Mitchell, you win. I am issuing an order to remove the Mexican nationals from the Imperial Valley today."

Elated, I called the Farm Labor Union office in El Centro to relay the good news, and was told the strike had been called off and the melon-pickers were headed north. While the melon-growers had lost their crop, the union had won an empty victory at the Labor Department in Washington, because the time for the harvest was over.

Farm labor organizing in California came to a dead stop. Hank Hasiwar was transferred to Louisiana where the action was. It was to be fifteen years before the rise of Cesar Chavez and the United Farm Workers of America.

The Strawberry Rebellion & the Cane Mutiny

Early in 1951, hundreds of small farmers swarmed out on the highways in Louisiana, forcibly stopping all strawberries going to market. They were receiving seven cents a box for strawberries that were sold in chain stores for twenty-five cents.

Even the Catholic Church was involved. Vincent O'Connell, Marist Priest and social action leader, was there as soon as the picketing of the highways got under way. The American Federation of Labor was called in, and I, as President of the National Farm Labor Union—an AFL affiliate—was asked to send in organizers. Hank Hasiwar soon arrived on the scene.

By then, the farmers had set up a cooperative marketing system, which they called a one-desk selling agency. A professional fruit and vegetable marketing agent was hired to handle the farmers' crops. The price of strawberries increased from $1.50 to $9 per crate of 24-pint boxes. The farmers, not the middlemen, reaped the profits.

Italians, Hungarians, French-speaking Cajuns, both whites and blacks were all represented on the forty-member Executive Board that met each day with the sales agent to decide the price for which the strawberries would be offered to buyers from chain-stores such as A & P and Safeway. Prior to the com-

Louisiana sugarcane plantation-workers on strike in 1953.

Above: *A sugarcane worker cutting cane by hand is a rare sight today.* Below: *This is one of the machines that has replaced hand-cutting of cane.*

ing of the union, chainstore buyers would meet in the coffee shop at Casa de Fresa Hotel and make such decisions regarding the price to be paid to the farmers. Now it was different. The farmers, all 3600 of them, were united.

Efforts were made to break the union. The small-town merchants and businessmen were in favor of the union. So were the majority of the handlers, the middlemen who, for a percentage of the price, packed and prepared the crates for shipment in refrigerated train and truck carloads. But some of the handlers refused to work with the union and its one-desk selling agency. The union put picketlines around their packing sheds. Some non-union trucks were loaded for shipment to market. The union pickets appeared. The fruitpackers got injunctions against the pickets. So the pickets' wives and children took over the picketlines, while the farmers stood aside and cheered them on.

Strawberry farmers Louis Edwards and Cassell Jones were jailed after they beat up a truckdriver who attempted to go through the picketlines. Conditions in the local jail—where they were held overnight—were so bad that the union appropriated money to to repair the place, in case other union men might be locked up. But no more were jailed.

Union Convicted of Anti-trust Act Violation

The chainstore buyers sought the help of the U.S. Department of Justice. The FBI investigated the farmers and their union operation in Louisiana. The 1952 Presidential election campaign was under way. The union set up a Political Action Committee. The strawberry farmers and their friends voted almost 100% for Adlai Stevenson, and Louisiana went

Democratic by a few thousand votes, but General Eisenhower won.

An anti-trust suit against the union was started by the new Attorney General, Herbert Brownell, as soon as he assumed office. There was another anti-trust action pending in the U.S. Department of Justice—against General Motors. Charles Wilson, President of General Motors, had become a cabinet member in the Eisenhower administration. He announced the slogan: ''What's good for General Motors is good for America.'' The anti-trust suit against the billion-dollar corporation was dropped. The union had only me in Washington, and my influence was nil when the ''Gold Cadillac Crusade'' led by General Ike started to roll.

Action against the 3600 little farmers was prosecuted. Judge Herbert S. Christenberry of the U.S. District Court refused to accept a settlement worked out in Washington by the union lawyers and the Anti-Trust Division of the Department of Justice. Instead, this judge—later to be hailed for his precedent-setting civil rights decisions—imposed fines and prison sentences on the union and on the officers of the local. Hank Hasiwar, who had led a strike of sugarcane fieldworkers, was given the heaviest fine and most severe sentence. He was placed on probation for five years, and forbidden to take part in union work.

The Cane Mutiny of 1953

While the above case was still pending settlement, the union—with the open support of rural priests of the powerful Catholic Church—started organizing the sugarcane fieldworkers on the plantations of South Louisiana. For several years, sugar refinery workers had been unionized by the CIO, and even a few of

the seasonal sugarcane grinding mills were covered by a union contract setting wages and other conditions of employment. The cane fieldworkers felt that they too should be treated the same way, but in spite of the intervention of the Archbishop of New Orleans in behalf of the union, the owners and managers of the sugarcane corporations refused even to meet or to discuss a settlement of the fieldworkers' demands, and defied Archbishop Rummel.

The workers voted to go on strike. The sugar establishment retaliated by securing state court injunctions prohibiting strikes during the harvest season. (This outrageous prohibition had been proposed even earlier by Congressman Richard M. Nixon.) Of greater importance to the workers were massive firings and evictions of sugar fieldworker

Strawberry farmers' picketline in Hammond, Louisiana, 1953. In the center is Hank Hasiwar, vice-president of the National Agricultural Workers' Union—AFL.

Above: *100 Self-Help Homes were built by the Union in Louisiana between 1965 and 1970. Here the children of Mr and Mrs Robert Moore play leapfrog while (r. to l.) H. L. Mitchell, Frank Lapayrolerie and Mr and Mrs Moore look on.* Far right: *Former slave quarters on the San Francisco plantation in Reserve, Louisiana, in 1967. Buildings like this were still occupied by farm workers in the mid-1970s. (Photo by Betsy Burleson)* Right: *Self-Help housing under construction, with Union sponsorship, for the use of sugarcane plantation-workers. (Photo by Lynn Franklin)*

families. I wanted to do as the STFU had done in the early battles in Arkansas, which was to defy the court injunctions and let them fill the jails with strikers. When strikebreakers were brought in from other areas, the trucks were fired on. There was also violence when strikebreakers, led by a CIO organizer, were brought into the refineries, which were being picketed by fieldworkers.

As soon as the strike started, Archbishop Rummel called in Hank Hasiwar and put him through a questioning that would have done credit to the grand inquisitor of the Spanish Inquisition. Hank, exhausted, finally asked: "Dammit, your Excellency, whose side are you on anyway?" Then the Archbishop asked how much would be needed in strike funds to make sure that none of the strikers' families went hungry or lacked shelter during the strike. Hank did some rapid calculations and suggested that a minimum of $7,000 would be needed during the first two weeks, while the union office was getting out an appeal for funds to other unions. The Archbishop instructed him where to go to pick up the money, which was handed to him in a paper bag. In his excitement, Hank left the bag on the back seat of his car while he went into a beerjoint on the road, to have a beer. Suddenly, realizing what he had done, Hank rushed out in a panic, but found the sack undisturbed, and carried it to the bank before closing time.

During this critical time, the Rev. Vincent J. O'Connell, one of the principal organizers of the sugarcane workers' revolt, was transferred to a very large church in St. Paul, Minnesota.

The case of the Cane Mutiny ended in the highest court in the land. The U.S. Supreme Court agreed to hear the cane-workers' appeal on a paupers' oath. A young Washington lawyer, Daniel Pollitt, wrote

Left to right: *Robert Carter, child-care specialist; Lorna Bourg, assistant to the director of the Southern Mutual Help Association; Rev. Murphy Wright, SMHA board member; and Sister Anne Catherine, Rural Dominican nun and SMHA director.*

the brief, Dorothy Dowe Mitchell cut the stencil, and I ran it off on the mimeograph machine. All three of us carried it to the clerk of the Supreme Court to be filed. Two years later, though the question was then moot, the U.S. Supreme Court ordered the Louisiana courts to set aside the injunction prohibiting strikes during harvest time.

The AFL-CIO is Persuaded to Help Organize Farm Workers

Prior to the merger of the AFL and the CIO in 1956, Walter Reuther, President of the United Auto Workers, told us that once the merger was brought about, he would see that the labor movement launched a campaign to organize the nation's farm workers. In 1959, the AFL-CIO agreed to finance a drive to organize the nation's farm workers.

Supported by early civil-rights leader A. Philip Randolph and by Reuther inside the AFL-CIO, and

Right: *Frank Lapeyrolerie, leader of the Louisiana sugarcane plantation-workers, shown here speaking for sugarcane workers at a U. S. Department of Agriculture wage hearing in Houma, Louisiana, 1969.* Above: *Louisiana Self-Help Housing, sponsored by the Union.*

with Frank Graham, Norman Thomas and Mrs Roosevelt bringing outside pressure to bear, plans were made by our union. Jack Livingston, the AFL-CIO Organization Director, proposed an initial appropriation of $150,000. I felt that this was too much, but accepted the proposal, expecting the AFL-CIO Council to reduce it by half. However, they appropriated the full amount. Stockton, California was selected as the place to launch the new AFL-CIO Agricultural Workers Organizing Committee.

George Meany, President of the AFL-CIO, never could see any profit in organizing people as poor as farm workers, and found me personally obnoxious for insisting that Labor help in doing so. Meany told Walter Reuther that he would not have Mitchell involved in the new AFL-CIO effort, even as a file clerk. Norman Smith, an old-time auto worker, was selected to head the Committee. Ernesto Galarza was named as Smith's assistant, but he lasted in that position less than a year.

The drive was launched with fanfare in the news media. Little progress was made during the first four years. Organizers and leaders trained in the NFLU were nearly all replaced by inexperienced people from other fields. Then a group of Filipino workers who had struck the Schenley ranch at Delano about twelve years before, under NFLU auspices, led by Philip Vera Cruz,went out again. Cesar Chavez, who was then operating an organization in Delano as a service center for farm workers, assumed leadership of the Agricultural Workers Organizing Committee, and the United Farm Workers of America came into existence. The Southern Tenant Farmers' Union, and its successor organizations, had been the forerunner, fighting many battles over many years and paving the way for Cesar Chavez and the United Farm Workers.

Down South Again

In mid-1960 the remnants of what was then called the National Agricultural Workers Union merged with the Amalgamated Meat Cutters and Butcher Workmen of North America, one of the largest unions in the AFL-CIO. I became their Agricultural Representative, and started work anew in the South. Seeking to revive the movement in Arkansas and other mid-southern states where the STFU had had its origins, I soon realized that times had changed. The sharecroppers had all left the farms. The modern day tenant farmer was often an operator of several thousands of acres, using machinery valued at half a million dollars, and very few farm-machine operators were required.

I turned my attention to Louisiana, where remnants of the movement still existed on dairy farms and in plants as well as on sugar plantations. Determined not to repeat the mistakes of the past, the union launched a drive to provide education, housing and health care for sugarcane plantation workers. Self-help housing was built for many who were still living in cabins once occupied by their slave forebears. Some success in organizing dairy plant employees was attained.

Organizing the Sharecroppers of the Sea

A new, quite militant group now came to the union for assistance. Their slogan was, "Git that extra man off my back." I promptly dubbed them "sharecroppers of the sea," for they were paid wages based on a share of the fish caught by the crew of a seventeen-man boat. The catch was that the fishermen were required to pay a part of their share to hire extra men, who were seldom even on the boat, and they believed the union offered a way to get rid of that extra man

Menhaden fishing fleet at anchor. Menhaden are fish commonly called "pogies," and the fishermen are known as "pogy-boat" men.

"The Face of the Fisherman": Howard V. Harrity in 1965 (photo by Lynn Franklin).

they were paying from their hard-earned wages. Since they were classed as industrial workers, the National Labor Relations Board conducted elections on each boat. Fifty-four elections were held in 1964, and the union won fifty-one of them.

Soon after the elections were won, I received a telephone call. Thinking my caller was a newspaperman, I launched into an account of what had happened. The caller said he had been the lawyer for the fishermen's union on the East Coast, and thought he could help us get contracts with the principal employer of the menhaden fishermen. It turned out that the caller was also a politico who had just been elected Chief Executive of Baltimore County, and was to go even further. His name was Spiro T. Agnew, later Richard Nixon's Vice-President. Both almost—but not quite—made it to prison. I afterward referred to Ted Agnew as "an honest crook, who just wanted as much money as he could get, while Nixon tried to steal the whole country and subvert its institutions."

It turned out that Ted Agnew was instrumental in helping the union to get contracts with the principal employer of fishermen and fish-plant workers. Millionaire Otis H. Smith, whose family owned many of the plants and fish boats, and Howard Harrity, soon worked out agreements satisfactory to all. The fishermen won their struggle to "Git that extra man off my back." The fish plant workers were organized, too, and now operate under union contracts.

Tenant farmers union remembers bold past

By WILLIAM SERRIN
NEW YORK TIMES SERVICE

Southern Tenant Farmers Union

Farmers Union Plans Program For Anniversary

The Southern Tenant Farmers Union will celebrate ...s 50th anniversary with a program from 9 a.m. to 5 p.m. Friday in the Old State House at 300 West Markham Street.

GOLDEN ANNIVERSARY

Sharecroppers' Union Celebrates 48th Anniversary Of 'Revolution'

12A ARKANSAS DEMOCRAT • SATURDAY, MARCH 10, 1984 •

Historic farm union to mark anniversary

BY CARL T. HALL
Democrat Staff Writer

The 50th anniversary of the founding of the historic Southern Tenant Farmers Union ...ill be...

The union went on to become famous for its often bitter struggles to organize black and white sharecroppers into the same union.

The STARS and STRIPES
AUTHORIZED U...
Vol. 42 No. ...

Tenant farmers' movement:
'Never just a union'

Page 10-K   The SUNDAY EXPRESS-NEWS, San Antonio, March 25, 1984

Tenant farmers union

Out of Our Past:
Some STFU Anniversaries

A Documentary Film on the STFU

After my autobiography was published in 1979, Alexander H. Schullman, the union's attorney in its California operation, contacted friends in the motion picture industry, whom he had also represented, to see if they could not be interested in making a movie of *Mean Things Happening in This Land*. One of the topflight producers is reported to have said: ''This thing is like *Roots* [Alex Haley's famed book about Black people] and would cost $20-million to make.''

Hollywood just was not that interested. With the help of friends who had contacts in public broadcasting, and in education, a proposal was put forth to make a documentary film of the struggle of farm workers to organize. This film is being completed as this book goes to press. The story of how the nation's farm workers built a union is at last available on film as well as in print.

Anniversary Celebrations

Beginning in 1959, there have been anniversary celebrations of the founding of the now historic Southern Tenant Farmers' Union. Here is the story of these celebrations, in brief.

In 1959, the 25th Anniversary of the founding of the Southern Tenant Farmers' Union was celebrated in Memphis, and Norman Thomas was the principal speaker. Among the messages sent by great Americans to the STFU at this meeting, was one from Eleanor Roosevelt:

It seems fitting that those of us who are concerned with the problems of the two million families who work on the nation's farms should be together and participate in the celebration of the 25th anniversary of the organization of these people who seek to express their God-given right to human dignity.

Beale Street, Memphis: "Where the blues was born."

In April 1982, the remaining members of the now historic Southern Tenant Farmers' Union called its 48th Anniversary Meeting. Less than forty members were there to take part, but over two hundred people from the academic field as well as from organized labor and community organizations were there to learn from the past. They attended a two-day meeting at Memphis, at the historic First Baptist Church on Beale Street. Four thousand feet of color film were shot, and twenty-three individuals were interviewed on videotape, for later use in the documentary film, and as research material by scholars interested in the subject. Some of the young visitors were so enthused with the proceedings of the meeting and its participants, that they demanded that it become an annual event. It was decided that we hold a 50th Anniversary Meeting.

At the Old State House, Little Rock

Prior to the meeting on March 16, 1984, the New York *Times* ran a half-page article about the STFU and H. L. Mitchell, which was widely reprinted. The newspaper of the armed forces, *The Stars and Stripes*, reprinted it, using the headline: "Tenant Farmers' Movement—Never Just a Union." This advance publicity attracted more attention from the mass media than was expected. It resulted in local radio, press and TV coverage, but of even more interest was the attention given by the National TV News. Several camera crews recorded it all. Said the National Public Radio program, ''All Things Considered,'' heard all over the world:

The 50th anniversary of the country's first farm worker union was celebrated in Little Rock. . . . Historians say that the Southern Tenant Farmers' Union helped farm workers more than anything since the Homestead Act (adopted 1862 during Lincoln's administration). An integrated group of farm tenants and sharecroppers formed the union to fight what many people say today was legalized slavery. George Stith was one of the youngest members of the group, at age 18, and says he and other farm workers were exploited. ''A sharecropper was one who the plantation owner furnished the land, the mule and a plow, the feed and the seed. You did all the work, and when the product made, mostly cotton, you carried it to the gin. You were supposed to get half of what was made, but you didn't get half. The plantation owner kept the records. He sold the cotton and told you what you made, and that was mostly more credit at the plantation store.''

Plantation owners fought the idea of a union, and Stith claims violence was the primary weapon:

''A few got killed. Many got beaten. Others were thrown in jail. I was never thrown in jail, but I was threatened many times. Many times I had to swim the canals and streams, full of snakes, at night, to get away after we had a meeting. We forgot about the danger, trying to make living conditions better.''

John L. Handcox, folksinger, was identified as one of the leaders, and had to leave the state:

''I had to leave Arkansas. I heard them talking about me. They said, 'We got a rope and we got a limb, and all we need is John Handcox.' If they could stop me, they could defeat the union.''

In spite of the beatings, the Southern Tenant Farmers' Union continued to organize. A union investigation was conducted by a Little Rock minister and a white woman from Memphis, and both were beaten up. Co-founder of the union, H. L. Mitchell says that incident did as much as anything for the union effort:

''The whole country was aroused. The idea of a white woman in the South being beaten! They didn't give a damn about a black woman being beaten. Eliza Nolden, black, was beaten so bad she died, because she joined a march through the plantations. A white woman, member of a prominent family in Memphis!

A. E. Cox, Secretary of the STFU and founder of the Delta and Providence cooperative farms, shown here holding the STFU's 25th Anniversary Journal.

Even local newspapers were outraged. It was only a few weeks before the President moved to set up a Farm Tenant Committee. Within a year, the Farm Security Administration was set up, and made loans and formed cooperatives. The Agency gave benefits to thousands of low-income families, including tenant farmers and sharecroppers.''

A Look to the Future

The solution to the farm problem does not lie in trying to turn back the clock to the eighteenth century ideal of small farm ownership. It remains the same as it was in the 1930s when we in the STFU had a dream that large-scale privately-owned plantations could be made into cooperative farming units owned and operated by and for the farmers who did the actual work on the land. Instead, the farms, ranches and plantations have grown larger. The land is owned by corporate enterprises whose objective is to make a huge profit. For over fifty years they have been subsidized by the U.S. Treasury. Labor from Mexico and the West Indies has been provided, while labor-displacing machines have been developed by other agencies of government. The taxpayer and consumer have paid for the capital investment in land, machinery and labor a hundred times over.

Farm workers today, like workers in all the multinational industries, need a multinational union in order to win. Eventually agriculture, our largest industry, must be socialized and operated for the benefit of those who work on the land and those who consume its products. This I believe is the real wave of the future.

The tradition of the Southern Tenant Farmers' Union is carried on today by the United Farm Workers of America, the Farm Labor Organizing Committee and community organizations like ACORN all over the USA. The memory of the Southern Tenant Farmers' Union lives on in the songs of union troubadour John Handcox:

> *We're gonna roll, we're gonna roll,*
> *We're gonna roll the Union on;*
> *We're gonna roll, we're gonna roll,*
> *We're gonna roll the Union on.*
>
> *If the boss is in the way,*
> *We're gonna roll it over him;*
> *We're gonna roll the Union on.*

John L. Handcox, George Stith and H. L. Mitchell

That Damned Mitchell Again

Since that hot night in July 1934, when eighteen men met to form the Southern Tenant Farmers' Union, I have never known what it was to be bored. I have been tired, sometimes I have been discouraged, and sometimes I have been very angry. I have never met a man or a woman that I could not really have liked. I could not hate the plantation-owners of eastern Arkansas, or their retainers who often wanted to take my life, and a few times damned near succeeded. I could not hate the deputy sheriffs or the plantation riders who broke up union meetings, beat up men and women, and even killed a few. I felt sorry for them all, for they too were the victims of a system they did not make. I could never hate the politicians who supported or the bureaucrats who administered the programs that had built-in discrimination against those who were at the bottom of the economic heap. However, I have always believed that it was my job, no matter where I was, to expose injustice, to stir up controversy among complacent people. I believe that if "mean things" are brought to light, then something may eventually be done to correct them.

I don't believe there is another world to come, and I am glad there isn't—to live to be one hundred is enough. I have never accumulated any of this world's goods. I never built a lasting organization of people; I never had the problem of exercising power justly because I never had any power. There will be no marble-faced building erected to the memory of H. L. Mitchell in Washington or anywhere else, and I am glad.

When I shall have lived out my life (100 years, more or less), I have asked that my body be cremated, and that my ashes be scattered in the wind over eastern Arkansas. Then, if any one of the plantation owners or their descendants who know of me still survive, may they some day look up to the sky, and if something gets in their eyes, they can then say: "There is that damned Mitchell again."

"That damned Mitchell again!"

THE S.T.F.U. NEWS

The Sharecroppers Voice
"The Voice Of The Disinherited"

The Farm Worker
Published by the Southern Tenant Farmers Union

The Tenant Farmer
Published Monthly by the
SOUTHERN TENANT FARMERS UNION
Perkins Bldg., 66 South Third Street
Memphis, Tenn.
Subscription Rate 50c per Year

FARM LABOR NEWS

Vol. 2. No. 12.   Memphis, Tenn.   December, 1947   25¢ Per Year

THE AGRICULTURAL UNIONIST

ol 1, No. 1   16   Washington, D.C.   August, 1952

The official publications of the STFU and its successors were lively rank-and-filers' papers, and characteristically included songs and poems—and plenty of humor—along with news, editorials and "official business."

Songs & Poems of the STFU

KING COTTON

The planters celebrated King Cotton in Memphis, May fifteen.
It was the largest gathering you most ever seen.
People came from far and near—to celebrate King Cotton
Whom the planters love so dear.
Thousands of flags were hung in the street,
But they left thousands of sharecroppers on their farms with nothing
*   to eat.*
Why do they celebrate Cotton? Here, I'll make it clear:
Because they cheat, beat and take it away from labor every year.

Cotton is King, and will always be,
Until labor in the South is set free.
The money spent for decorations and flags,
Would sure have helped poor sharecroppers who are hungry and in
*   rags.*
Oh! King Cotton, today you have millions of slaves
And have caused many poor workers to be in lonesome graves.
When Cotton is King of any nation,
It means wealth to the planter—to the laborer starvation.

John L. Handcox

SHERIFF PEACHER'S STOCKADE

We had heard about it, of course;
Rumor sketched the inmates clearly—
*   Their alarm, their rage,*
*   Penned in the coop*
*   Till dawn-work-morning.*

We trudged up a bent path—
The fossil grass limp, puffs
Of cotton dangling. . .
*   We smelled danger.*

*   Then came upon*
Friends: purple, white, jaune—
*   Gerard; my dear;*

Others—we are of all
*   These people, who*
*   Traveled so far. . .*
*   I do remember.*

Barbara Howes

STRIKE IN ARKANSAS

The day labor called a strike the eighteenth day of May,
For they cannot live on what the planters pay.
They asked the people in Memphis not to go out on the truck,
But the picketers found that jail was their luck.
The Union having many friends and good support had to pay
A ten dollar fine to the unjust Memphis Court.

Arkansas family, 1935.

In Earle, Arkansas they threw so many in jail,
That anyone would class such arrest as "wholesale."
Some planters have forced the labor into the field with gun,
And are driving them like convicts from sun to sun.
The planter is using pistols and whipping labor across the head,
Telling them "If you don't get in my field, I kill you dead."

The Planter say to ask for a dollar and a half a day is unfair,
They never mention high prices the labor have to pay him for what
    he eat and wear.
Everybody knows the Union isn't asking for enough,
If we remember how the planter sells his beans and stuff.
They're riding around cussing and raising sand,
When it's known they sold the 25-cent-size baking powder for 50 cents
    a can.

They arrested Mr Gilmartin, a New York guest,
Who was investigating the people who were in distress.
On May Twenty-second, the most terrible thing happen you ever could
    record.
Peacher attacked Miss Evelyn Smith and Mrs Clay East,
Told them to leave there at once for they were disturbing the peace.
They went out to take a picture of Union people he had in the Stockade,
Only wanting to seek some way to give the Union people aid.
Peacher took their kodak, and tore up their film,
Saying, "You'd better leave Arkansas, or you be hung to a limb."
The planter law in Arkansas is raising Cain,
They have no respect for person—woman or man.

If you go through Arkansas, you better drive fast,
How the labor is being treated, you better not ask.
I warn you to give enough money to give bail,
For if planter law find you in sympathy with labor, they put you in jail.
It make no difference, whether white or black,
If you all in the ring, you look all alak.

John Handcox

In Arkansas—The Wonder State

"This is the first chance I have had to enjoy the generosity, the kindness and the courtesy of true Arkansas hospitality."
—Franklin D. Roosevelt

President Roosevelt's visit to Arkansas in 1936 was not particularly appreciated by the STFU, as this cartoon from the July 1936 issue of the union's official paper, The Sharecroppers' Voice, *plainly shows.*

Coming in to Memphis
(From Marked Tree)

This-here is the end of a world,
Full of the gloomy and endless wailing
Of the propertyless great-grandchildren of slaves.
Poverty here tooths the eroded banks,
Silts up the furrows with sand,
Picks at the boards of cabins.
This is the end of my kind of world.
Oh Challengers,
Oh Movers of the new thing in the human spirit,
Is it the beginning of yours?

Naomi Mitchison

Goodbye to the Southern Tenant Farmers Union

We turn our backs on Marked Tree and the grim miles of cotton.
Forgive us, McKinney and Moskop, Brookins and Stultz, forgive—
You-all, think friendly of us, not quite gone and forgotten.
We are needing your forgiveness as you need to live.
Here we are, warm, well-fed, security round and through us
White like an English blanket, we running away.
Forgive us, Mitchell and Kester, who never knew us,
Only the faces we turned you, the talk of a day.
We with our pound-bought dollars, each in turn buying
Romance or beauty or struggle, all there is to be had,
Now they carry us safe off, while you maybe are dying.
Forgive us our trespasses, we sure do need it bad.

Naomi Mitchison
(with Zita Baker)

WE BELIEVE

We believe
That a gun is no defense
In the hands of a hungry man.
That battleships are no defense for a people ill-housed.
That anti-aircraft guns are no defense
Against the poisonous fumes of discontent and disillusion.
These are the things we believe:
That a free nation is one whose people gain each year
More share in all its goods.
That free speech, free press, voting, free assembly
Are but the framework of democracy,
The sturdy props on which we build
The strong, the spacious House
With room for all,
With work and food for all,
With full security,
With space for growing.
We have the sturdy props,
We have the ground-plan,
The building is begun.
We have a stake in its completion.
The building must go on.
This is our defense,
This is our democracy.
This is our land.

Harriet Young

A Vassar graduate active in the Socialist Party, Harriet Young was the STFU's eastern U.S. representative and helped coordinate National Sharecroppers Week in 1938 and '39. Later she was educational director of the International Ladies Garment Workers Union in Ohio and taught at the Hudson Shore Labor School in New York.

HUNGRY, HUNGRY ARE WE

Hungry, hungry are we,
Just as hungry as hungry can be,
We don't get nothin' for our labor,
So hungry, hungry are we.

Raggedy, raggedy are we,
Just as raggedy as raggedy can be.
We don't get nothin' for our labor,
So raggedy, raggedy are we.

Homeless, homeless are we,
Just as homeless as homeless can be.
We don't get nothin' for our labor,
So homeless, homeless are we.

Landless, landless are we,
Just as landless as landless can be.
We don't get nothin' for our labor,
So landless, landless are we.

John L. Handcox

BALLAD OF THE
DI GIORGIO STRIKERS

Pickets standing on the line
Looking down the country road,
Saw a lonesome stranger coming
And he said his name was Joad.

Now the stranger stood beside us
And his face was pale and thin,
Said he'd like to join the Union
So we said we'd let him in.

Thursday night he came to meeting
And he raised his snowy head,
With a voice like Resurrection
Spoke, and this is what he said:

"There's a fence around Creation,
There's a mortgage on the sun,
They have put electric meters
Where the rivers used to run."

"God Almighty made the valley
For a land of milk and honey,
But a corporation's got it
For to turn it into money."

Ernesto Galarza

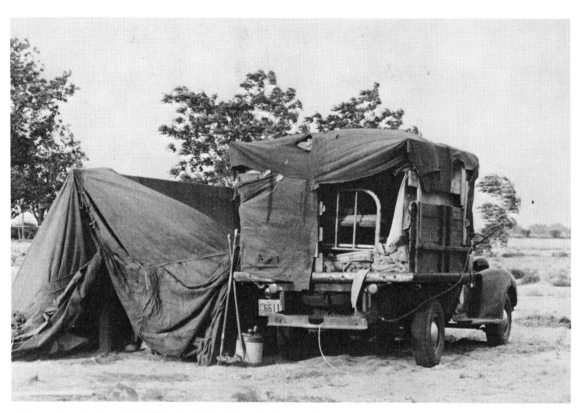

A farm laborer's home in California, 1954. (Photo by Ernesto Galarza)

Red Emma Passes at Toronto

Red Emma passes at Toronto, the newspapers say.
But the death of a woman of seventy
Is scarcely news today,
When cities are bombed and rivers of red
Are flowing and workers are dying across the sea.

Who was Emma Goldman and why did they call her red,
Why, she was hardly a lady even by the standard of today,
Though once she was young and beautiful, that too had passed away.
Not long ago she stirred workers to thinking
And that was the reason she was red.

Red Emma was proud of that title, which she held to her dying day.
This great woman was deported, America should claim her today.
For war and its carnage she hated, and always raised her voice to say
That American workers had nothing whatever to gain that way.
She stirred people to thinking and that was the reason she was a Red.

Emma Goldman knew no master, no one ever possessed her.
And in prison as in exile she bowed to no authority.
She held no beliefs but one and that was—people should be free.
In a world that is in shambles and tyrants triumphantly have their way
We are better off now for the free spirit of Emma Goldman is alive
*   even today.*

> *So Red Emma passes at Toronto, the newspapers say.*
> *But the death of a woman of seventy*
> *Is scarcely news today,*
> *For cities are bombed and rivers of blood*
> *Are flowing and workers are dying across the sea.*

H. L. Mitchell

Written upon reading about the death of Russian-born anarchist Emma Goldman (1869-1940). Deported from the United States because of her opposition to World War I and later persecuted in Russia by the Bolsheviks, she lived much of her later life in Europe. Her autobiography, *Living My Life*, is one of the most remarkable documents of all time.

ROLL THE UNION ON

It was nineteen hundred and thirty six
And on the 18th day of May,
When the STFU pulled a strike
That troubled the planters on their thrones.

The planters they all became troubled,
Not knowing what 'twas all about,
But they said, ''One thing I'm sure we can do,
That's scare them sharecroppers out.''

We're gonna roll, we're gonna roll,
We're gonna roll the Union on;
We're gonna roll, we're gonna roll,
We're gonna roll the Union on.

If the planter's in the way,
We're gonna roll it over him,
We're gonna roll it over him,
We're gonna roll it over him,
We're gonna roll the Union on.

If the boss is in the way,
We're gonna roll it over him,
We're gonna roll the Union on.

If the governor's in the way,
We're gonna roll it over him,
We're gonna roll the Union on.

John L. Handcox

Some STFU old-timers at the Fortieth Anniversary Celebration at Little Rock, 1974. Left to right: A. E. Cox, George Stith, Evelyn Smith Munro, Lindsey Cox, Sidney Hertzberg, Frank Lapeyrolie and Clay East.

Covington Hall, organizer of the Louisiana-based Brotherhood of Timber Workers, also editor and poet of the Industrial Workers of the World, once wrote a poem that went something like this:

Sloughfoot Sam and his gal, Lou,
Rode up thar on a kangaroo.
You've seen yore share of Hell on Earth
Said old St. Pete,
So come right in and rest a spell,
Cause you paid more rent and interest, too,
Than God in Heaven can count for you.

Further Reading

Ameringer, Oscar. *If You Don't Weaken: The Autobiography of Oscar Ameringer.* Norman: University of Oklahoma Press, 1983. Reprint of 1938 edition with a new introduction by James R. Green.

Brommel, Bernard C. *Eugene V. Debs: Spokesman for Labor and Socialism.* Chicago: Charles H. Kerr Publishing Company, 1978.

Burton, Orville Vernon. *In My Father's House Are Many Mansions.* Chapel Hill: University of North Carolina Press, 1985.

Cantor, Louis. *Prologue to the Protest Movement.* Durham: Duke University Press, 1967.

Conrad, David. *Forgotten Farmers.* Urbana: University of Illinois Press, 1967.

Dunbar, Anthony P. *Against the Grain: Southern Radicals and Prophets.* Charlottesville: University of Virginia Press, 1981.

Dunne, John Gregory. *Delano: The Story of the California Grape Strike.* New York: Farrar, Straus & Giroux, 1967.

Fusfeld, Daniel R. *The Rise and Repression of Radical Labor in the United States, 1877-1918.* Chicago: Charles H. Kerr Publishing Company, 1985.

Galarza, Ernesto. *Farm Workers and Agri-Business in California, 1947-1960.* Notre Dame: University of Notre Dame Press, 1977.

—:*Merchants of Labor.* Santa Barbara: McNally & Lofton, 1964.

—: *Spiders in Our House and Workers in the Field.* Notre Dame: University of Notre Dame Press, 1970.

Goldman, Emma. *Living My Life.* New York: Dover, 1970.

Goodwyn, Lawrence. *Democratic Promise: The Populist Movement in America.* New York: Oxford University Press, 1978.

Green, James R. *Grass Roots Socialism.* Baton Rouge: Louisiana State University Press, 1978.

Grubbs, Donald H. *Cry from the Cotton: The Southern Tenant Farmers Union and the New Deal.* Chapel Hill: University of North Carolna Press, 1971.

Guerin, Daniel. *100 Years of Labor in the USA.* London: InkLinks, 1970.

Hall, Covington. *Dreams and Dynamite: Selected Poems.* Edited and introduced by Dave Roediger. Chicago: Charles H. Kerr Publishing Company, 1985.

Jameson, Stuart. *Labor Unionism in American Agriculture.* Washington: Bureau of Labor Statistics No. 836, U. S. Department of Labor.

Kester, Howard. *Revolt Among the Sharecroppers.* New York: Covici-Friede, 1936. Reprinted 1969 by Arno Press, New York.

Kornbluh, Joyce. *Rebel Voices: An IWW Anthology.* Introduction and Bibliographical Afterword by Fred Thompson. Chicago: Charles H. Kerr Publishing Company, 1987.

Lens, Sidney. *The Labor Wars: From the Molly Maguires to the Sitdowns.* New York: Doubleday Anchor, 1974.

London, Joan and **Henry Anderson:** *So Shall Ye Reap: The Story of Cesar Chavez and the Farm Workers' Movement.* New York: Crowell, 1970.

Marshall, Ray. *Labor in the South.* Cambridge: Harvard University Press, 1967.

Meister, Dick and **Anne Nevins Loftis.** *A Long Time Coming: The Struggle to Unionize American Farm Workers.* New York: Macmillan, 1979.

Mitchell, H. L. *Mean Things Happening in This Land: The Life and Times of H. L. Mitchell.* Towata: Rowman and Allanheld, 1979.

Nelson, Eugene. *Huelga: The First Hundred Days of the Great Delano Grape Strike.* Delano: Farm Worker Press, 1966.

Thomas, Norman. *The Plight of the Sharecropper.* New York: League for Industrial Democracy, 1934.

Thompson, Fred. *The IWW: Its First Seventy Years.* Chicago: Industrial Workers of the World, 1976.

—: *World Labor Needs a Union.* Chicago: Industrial Workers of the World, 1969.

Yellen, Samuel. *American Labor Struggles, 1877-1934.* New York: Monad Press, 1974.

* * *

See also the *Archives of the Rural Poor: the STFU Papers (1934-1970*, plus supplements, available on microfilm at many American libraries.

For information on the new documentary film, *Our Land Too: The Legacy of the STFU,* see the copyright page of this book.

Other Books from America's Oldest Labor Publisher

MEMOIRS OF A WOBBLY
by Henry E. McGuckin
At last—the *inside story* of the Industrial Workers of the World: how they hoboed, how they agitated, how they organized, how they waged their celebrated free-speech fights and their world-famous strikes. Written by a pre-World-War-I IWW organizer, this rank-and-file account of "building the new society in the shell of the old"—complete with a chapter on IWW agricultural workers' organizing in the 1910s—is a genuine labor classic. Includes a 1914 article by McGuckin from the *International Socialist Review*, and an Afterword on the author's later life by his son, Henry McGuckin, Jr. $6.95

THE FLIVVER KING: A Story of Ford-America
by Upton Sinclair
Sinclair's finest novel—the classic tale Ford, Fordism and the origins of the United Auto Workers, originally published in 1937 and long out of print. "The Flivver King *helped found our union. Ford workers read this book aloud to their families*"—Walter Reuther. "*An ideal novel to hand someone who needs to be told how capitalism works and why we need unions*"—Fred Thompson, *Industrial Worker*. Introduction by Steve Meyer. $7.95

DREAMS & DYNAMITE: Selected Poems
by Covington Hall
"*A collection of poems by the organizer for the IWW Timber Workers, who used to make speeches at Arkansas rallies of the Southern Tenant Farmers' Union. New York City socialists were always afraid of Covington Hall, fearing that he would start a sharecropper riot. We youngsters used to gather around to hear him tell of the class wars he had been involved in when he was our age*"—H. L. Mitchell. Introduction by Dave Roediger. $3.95

LIFE & DEEDS OF UNCLE SAM
by Oscar Ameringer
The funniest book by one of the most popular labor writers of all time—"the Mark Twain of American Socialism." First published in 1909, it sold half a million copies by 1917 and was translated into fifteen languages. "*A labor classic. Explains U.S. economic history in a satirical style that makes more sense than history books many times its length*"—*Labor Notes*. Introduction by Paul Buhle. $3.95

RISE & REPRESSION OF RADICAL LABOR IN THE U.S.A.
by Daniel R. Fusfeld
A popular short history of American labor insurgency and government repression, from the strike wave of 1877 through Haymarket and the Pullman Strike to the heyday of the IWW before, during and immediately after World War I. An excellent introduction to American labor history. *Illustrated*. $3.95

HAYMARKET SCRAPBOOK: A Centennial Anthology
Edited by Dave Roediger & Franklin Rosemont
Profusely illustrated oversize compilation on the most world-reverberating event in American labor history: the Haymarket Tragedy of 1886-87. Original articles by today's top labor historians—including William J. Adelman, Carolyn Ashbaugh, Paul Avrich, Alan Dawley, Richard Drinnon, Philip Foner, Joseph Jablonski, Sid Lens, Fred Thompson & many others, as well as numerous reprints of hard-to-find reminiscences, poems and tributes by Oscar Ameringer, Edward Bellamy, Ralph Chaplin, Voltairine de Cleyre, Clarence Darrow, Eugene Debs, Emma Goldman, Sam Gompers, Mother Jones, Lucy Parsons, Carl Sandburg, Upton Sinclair, Art Young, Carlos Cortez and dozens more, plus major texts by the Chicago Martyrs themselves. "*A marvelous, massive, very important book*"—Studs Terkel. $14.95

REASONS FOR PARDONING THE HAYMARKET ANARCHISTS
by John Peter Altgeld
Gov. Altgeld's classic pardon message, long out of print but reissued at last in a fine new edition that also includes a warm tribute to Altgeld by Clarence Darrow and a new introduction by Leon M. Despres. "*The calmest, clearest, most incisive and most factual dissertation on that stirring case*" (Harry Barnard). $3.95

BYE! AMERICAN: The Labor Cartoons of Huck & Konopacki
A large-format collection of 150 great cartoons by today's greatest labor cartoonists! "*Syndicated to scores of labor publications throughout the U.S. and Canada, the cartoons of Gary Huck & Mike Konopacki have long been appreciated on picketlines, in workers' homes, at union halls, unemployment lines and cheese distribution sites. Bye! American now provides an opportunity for a broader audience to sample the political insight and razor-sharp wit of these outstanding labor artists*"—from the Introduction by Roger Bybee, editor of *The Racine Labor*. Texts by David Elsila, Franklin Wallick, Michael Funke, Randi Einbinder & David Ortleib, and a short history of labor cartoons by Franklin Rosemont. $7.95

THE AUTOBIOGRAPHY OF FLORENCE KELLEY
Edited & Introduced by Kathryn Kish Sklar
One of the outstanding figures in the history of the American labor movement, Florence Kelley was a major leader in the struggle for progressive labor and social legislation. A mainstay of Jane Addams' Hull-House, she was also Illinois' first Chief Factory Inspector—appointed by Gov. Altgeld in 1893. This important and engaging memoir is published here as a separate volume for the first time. "*A touching personal story of one of America's greatest reformers. . .a significant contribution to women's history*"—Mari Jo Buhle. $7.95

Send for our complete catalog.

Please add $1 postage for the first book, & fifty cents for each additional book.

Charles H. Kerr Publishing Company, 1740 West Greenleaf Avenue, Suite 7, Chicago, Illinois 60626

MEET THE STFU

Roll the Union On tells one of the most exciting and inspiring stories of the modern American labor movement: the story of the Southern Tenant Farmers' Union and its long and bitter struggle for a better life for the downtrodden sharecroppers and farmworkers of the South and West.

Founded near Tyronza, Arkansas, in 1934 by eleven white and seven black workers, within five years the STFU was organizing all across the South and counting its members in the tens of thousands. Reviving old IWW traditions of workers' solidarity and direct action as its members added many an innovation discovered in the course of new struggles, the STFU brought a luster all its own to the labor insurgency of the 1930s and '40s. The first fully-integrated multiracial union in the modern South, the STFU prefigured not only later farmworkers' unionization but also the civil rights agitation of the 1960s and the growing rank-and-file labor revolt of our own time.

In *Roll the Union On* we meet, in words and pictures, some of the most important, dynamic and colorful activists in the modern labor movement. Not the least impressive among them is the author, H. L. Mitchell himself—a lifelong deep-south socialist still actively championing the cause of workingclass emancipation on the speakers' circuit today.

Here is a dramatic first-hand account of the origins, the struggles, the strikes, the achievements, the humor, the songs and poems of Southern rural working men and women who had a great dream, and set out together to make that dream a reality.

H. L. Mitchell at the STFU office in Memphis, Tennessee, in 1938.
(Photo by Dorothea Lange)

Charles H. Kerr Publishing Company
Established 1886